The Jesus Bible

FOREVER

THE STORY OF GOD MAKING ALL THINGS RIGHT

Aaron Coe, Ph.D.
Series Writer & General Editor of *The Jesus Bible*

Matt Rogers, Ph.D.
Series Writer & Lead Writer of *The Jesus Bible*

**Harper*Christian*
Resources**

passionpublishing

The Jesus Bible Study Series: Forever
© 2024 by Passion Publishing

Published in Grand Rapids, Michigan, by HarperChristian Resources. HarperChristian Resources is a registered trademark of HarperCollins Christian Publishing, Inc.

Requests for information should be sent to customercare@harpercollins.com.

ISBN 978-0-310-15508-9 (softcover)
ISBN 978-0-310-15509-6 (ebook)

HarperChristian Resources titles may be purchased in bulk for church, business, fundraising, or ministry use. For information, please e-mail ResourceSpecialist@ChurchSource.com.

First printing July 2024 / Printed in the United States of America

CONTENTS

INTRODUCTION

You have a story.

Everyone does.

And while your story is unique, all of our stories are alike in some ways.

Every story has a beginning. We were born on a specific date and in a particular place in the world. From that time, we began to grow and emerge into the people we are today.

We also all have an end. There will be a date in the future—one that we do not yet know—when our time on this earth will be finished. These dates of our birth and death serve as the first and last pages of the story of our lives.

But for followers of Christ, the Bible reveals that the end of our story on this earth is actually the beginning of a brand-new story that will last forever.

Forever is a long time. It's hard to wrap our minds around something so vast. We might occasionally drift into thoughts about forever, especially when something momentous happens, but more often than not we focus on what is immediately in front of us. We live our lives and give little thought to what forever will be like or what we need to do to prepare for that time.

Of course, this is a naïve decision. Our lives are so short—like "a mist that appears for a little while and then vanishes" (James 4:14). It's strange how we find this to be true and yet time and time again fail to grasp its significance. A couple vows to love each other "till death do us part," and we consider the implications of that commitment. A baby is born, and we think all the life that is ahead of him or her. A close family member dies . . . and our thoughts turn to reflections of everything that person did on earth. Each time these things happen, we are moved from our complacency and reminded that we have a finite number of days in this world. This is why it's so important for us to think about forever from God's perspective.

Throughout *The Jesus Bible Study Series*, we have learned about the major "acts" in God's story. Starting with *Beginnings*, we saw how God fashioned a world and made people in his own image so they would know him, worship him, and fill the earth with his glory. But the first couple, Adam and Eve, rebelled against God and plunged the world into sin—a story told in *Revolt*. However, God did not abandon his people. He continued to pursue them with his love, promising a Savior would one day come to fix the problem that sin had created.

The early stages of this plan, as discussed in *People*, were told through the nation of Israel. God gave them his promises, his law, a sacrificial system, and a land in which they could worship him rightly. But like Adam and Eve before them, they rebelled against God's plan and found themselves mired in sin. They needed a Savior, which is exactly what God provided by sending his Son. As told in *Savior*, Jesus Christ was God in the flesh—the one who did for humanity what they could not do for themselves. He perfectly kept God's law and then, in an act of sheer love, died on behalf of sinners. He came back to life on the third day, forever defeating sin and death. God now offers salvation to those who trust in Jesus' work.

Those whom God saves—as described in *Church*—are placed in a community of other believers, where they give their lives for the sake of his mission in the world. In the church, people gather in worship of God and seek to spur one another on to treasure Jesus even more. They also scatter into the world on a strategic mission to declare and demonstrate the good news of Jesus. This is the church's mission until Jesus returns.

These are the five acts in God's great story that we have explored so far in this series: (1) **Beginnings**, (2) **Revolt**, (3) **People**, (4) **Savior**, and (5) **Church**. Now we will move into the final act: **Forever**. But as we do, we have to concede that many of the details in Scripture about our eternity are unclear. We certainly aren't told about everything that we will be doing in heaven. Yet God has not been completely silent on the matter—and what we do know is sufficient to help us glimpse the beauty of what God is doing and where this world is heading.

Given that *Forever* is the last chapter in the grand story of Scripture, you will likely notice some recurring themes that have been pointed out in other studies in the series. Remember that the Bible is really a collection of sixty-six books telling one single story. It describes God's plan to save sinners and fix the world through Jesus Christ. The journey to forever reminds us that God will finish what he started and make all things right again. He will get the glory he deserves.

— AARON & MATT

Lesson One

THE OTHER SIDE

"And I will put enmity between you and the woman, and between your offspring and hers; he will crush your head, and you will strike his heel."

GENESIS 3:15

I saw the Holy City, the new Jerusalem, coming down out of heaven from God, prepared as a bride beautifully dressed for her husband.

REVELATION 21:2

"Now this is eternal life:
that they know you,
the only true God,
and Jesus Christ."

JOHN 17:3

WELCOME

You can probably think back on some of your earliest aspirations and laugh at their naivety. What did you want to be when you grew up? Who did you think you would marry? Where would you live? What would you be doing on a day-to-day basis?

As a teenager, my heart beat in sync with the rhythm of the media and music industry. I wasn't just another face in the crowd; I was the kid who eagerly raised his hand to join the church's media ministry. I craved every opportunity to immerse myself in the world of visuals and sounds. Beyond the sanctuary, I cultivated a side hustle, capturing precious moments on video for weddings, each event a symphony of emotions and melodies.

When the time came for me to choose a path for higher education, I set my sights on one of the nation's premier institutions for the music and media business. The first day I stepped onto the campus, I could feel the energy of creativity coursing through its veins. But then, during a late-night recording session in the studio, reality struck me like a thunderbolt. I was surrounded by fellow students who lived and breathed for the art, and while I cherished the allure of the industry, my soul didn't burn with the same fervor. It was an epiphany in the dimly lit studio—my destiny was tuned to a different frequency, though I couldn't decipher it just yet. All I knew in that moment was that the music and media path wasn't mine to travel.

We can never know for certain what our futures will hold. We often set out on a certain path but then find that our priorities have shifted. Life's twists and turns in this flawed world can drastically redirect our course. This is why James admonishes us against any presumptions of control: "Now listen, you who say, 'Today or tomorrow we will go to this or that city, spend a year there, carry on business and make money.' Why, you do not even know what will happen tomorrow. . . . Instead, you ought to say, 'If it is the Lord's will, we will live and do this or that'" (James 4:13–15). Our destinies are in God's hands, subject to his divine will.

Yet this acknowledgment doesn't render us completely blind to what lies ahead. While the specifics of our individual journeys may remain veiled, God has granted us insight into the broader narrative of life. As Peter wrote, "His divine power has given us everything we need for a godly life through our knowledge of him who has called us by his own glory and goodness" (2 Peter 1:3). We can have hope today amidst the uncertainties of tomorrow.

1. What is one thing you would like to accomplish within the next ten years?

2. How is your life different now than you thought it would be ten years ago?

READ

A Glimpse of Our Tomorrow

In the maze of life's uncertainties, we can find solace in this timeless truth: "[God's] word is a lamp for my feet, a light on my path." (Psalm 119:105). God assures us that in the midst of the darkness of the unknown, his Word will illuminate our way forward, guiding each step with his divine wisdom and clarity. As we embark on the journey of faith, we take hold of this beacon of hope, trusting that it will faithfully lead us through every twist and turn, through every triumph and trial, until we reach the destination of God's perfect purpose for our lives.

We get a glimpse of this eternal destination in the book of Revelation. Early church tradition, dating back to the second century, states that the book was penned by John, the disciple of Christ. It is believed that John was exiled to the remote isle of Patmos during a time of persecution in the late first century AD under the rule of the Roman emperor Domitian. As he explains, "I, John . . . was on the island of Patmos because of the word of God and the testimony of Jesus. On the Lord's Day I was in the Spirit, and I heard behind me a loud voice like a trumpet, which said: 'Write on a scroll what you see'" (Revelation 1:9–11).

The vision John receives on "the Lord's Day" (Sunday) unveils the culmination of God's cosmic drama, depicting the final showdown between good and evil, light and darkness. It paints a vivid picture of the victory of Christ over all opposing forces, ushering in a new heaven and a new earth where righteousness reigns supreme.

Moreover, John's vision offers a glimpse into the glorious consummation of God's purposes, where every tear is wiped away and death is swallowed up in victory (see Isaiah 25:8; 1 Corinthians 15:54). It unveils the eternal relationship between God and his people, where we will reign with him forevermore (see 2 Timothy 2:12). Thus, the book of Revelation serves not only as a prophetic road map but also as a source of hope and encouragement, reminding us that no matter how turbulent the present may seem, God's purposes for the future are secure and unshakeable. This is especially evident in the following passage:

> ¹ Then I saw "a new heaven and a new earth," for the first heaven and the first earth had passed away, and there was no longer any sea. ² I saw the Holy City, the new Jerusalem, coming down out of heaven from God, prepared as a bride beautifully dressed for her husband. ³ And I heard a loud voice from the throne saying, "Look! God's dwelling place is now among the people, and he will dwell with them. They will be his people, and God himself will be with them and be their God. ⁴ 'He will wipe every tear from their eyes. There will be no more death' or mourning or crying or pain, for the old order of things has passed away."

⁵ He who was seated on the throne said, "I am making everything new!" Then he said, "Write this down, for these words are trustworthy and true."

⁶ He said to me: "It is done. I am the Alpha and the Omega, the Beginning and the End. To the thirsty I will give water without cost from the spring of the water of life. ⁷ Those who are victorious will inherit all this, and I will be their God and they will be my children.

Revelation 21:1-7

3. What are some ways that God's Word has been a lamp for your feet and a light for your path? How has it provided guidance in your life?

4. How does John describe the eternal dwelling place of all believers in Christ in Revelation 21:1-7? How does this passage give you hope?

The Current State of the World

John states that the vision he received was a "revelation from Jesus" given to show followers of Christ "what must soon take place" (Revelation 1:1). He adds, "Blessed is the one who reads aloud the words of this prophecy, and blessed are those who hear it and take to heart what is written in it, because the time is near" (verse 3). The "time" to which John refers is the end of the world. This is a vision of what God is doing and will do in the future.

Many of the descriptions that John relates in the book of Revelation can be difficult to interpret. They are filled with picturesque imagery that was meant to aid his readers in understanding God's future work. Debates rage about the exact meaning of these pictures, even among longtime biblical scholars, because John is attempting to describe something that is simply too vast for the human mind to comprehend. Even the most stunning of images—like the streets of gold (see Revelation 21:21)—seemingly point to a future world that is far better than anything we can imagine. Our best materials will simply pave the streets of this future city.

Often lost amidst the challenging themes of the book are the main points that John—and, in turn, God—want us to see. The most significant is that God wins. The Bible ends just like it began, with God ruling and reigning over the world he made.

Much has happened since the story of the Bible began. People have continually rebelled against God. They have built cities designed to harness their sin. They have committed every sort of evil imaginable. They have made a mockery of God's grace. Along the way, Satan, the enemy, has seemingly won victory after victory. He has led people astray. He has shipwrecked the faith of many. Entire nations have been judged by God because of their disobedience. Perhaps the apostle Paul best summed up the enemy's successes when he wrote:

> *1 As for you, you were dead in your transgressions and sins, 2 in which you used to live when you followed the ways of this world and of the ruler of the kingdom of the air, the spirit who is now at work in those who are disobedient. 3 All of us also lived among them at one time, gratifying the cravings of our flesh and following its desires and thoughts. Like the rest, we were by nature deserving of wrath.*
>
> Ephesians 2:1–3

This is a dire summary of the human condition. The world is broken. People are spiritually dead in their transgressions and sins. It seems as if the enemy—"the ruler of the kingdom of the air"—is winning. He is actively working in those who are disobedient toward God. Peter adds that he "prowls around like a roaring lion looking for someone to devour" (1 Peter 5:8). The situation seems bleak. But followers of Jesus have the assurance that "the old order of things" will pass away (Revelation 21:4).

Regardless of how bad things are in this world, we have God's promise, "Never will I leave you; never will I forsake you" (Hebrews 13:5).

5. Why is it important for Christians to understand that God wins in the end? What do you envision when you picture yourself ruling and reigning with Jesus?

6. When you look at the state of the world today, what evidence do you see that Satan is actively at work? In what ways does he seem to be winning?

Signs of God's Presence

The Bible reveals that followers of God have often needed this same kind of reassurance when facing their future. Consider the story of the Exodus. The Israelites had been living as slaves in Egypt, but God had miraculously delivered them, and now they were headed toward a new promised land. But as they journeyed through the wilderness, uncertainty loomed like a shadow. How could they know that God was leading them? The Lord provided the answer:

> *⁷ When Pharaoh let the people go, God did not lead them on the road through the Philistine country, though that was shorter. For God said, "If they face*

war, they might change their minds and return to Egypt." ¹⁸ So God led the
people around by the desert road toward the Red Sea. The Israelites went
up out of Egypt ready for battle.

¹⁹ Moses took the bones of Joseph with him because Joseph had made
the Israelites swear an oath. He had said, "God will surely come to your aid,
and then you must carry my bones up with you from this place."

²⁰ After leaving Sukkoth they camped at Etham on the edge of the desert.
²¹ By day the LORD went ahead of them in a pillar of cloud to guide them on
their way and by night in a pillar of fire to give them light, so that they could
travel by day or night. ²² Neither the pillar of cloud by day nor the pillar of fire
by night left its place in front of the people.

Exodus 13:17–22

Of all the signs that God provided to his people, none was as tangible and as consistent as the pillar of cloud by day and pillar of fire by night. These celestial markers were not mere phenomena but practical reminders of God's presence and guidance. He was the one divinely leading his people through the desolate wilderness toward the promised land.

In this way, the cloud and fire served as more than just navigational aids. They also symbolized God's faithfulness and steadfast love. In the scorching heat of the desert, the cloud shielded the Israelites from the oppressive sun, offering relief and protection. As night descended, the fiery pillar pierced the darkness, casting its warm glow upon the camp, warding off fear and uncertainty. These manifestations were tokens of God's unwavering commitment to his people, guiding them through the wilderness of life with divine precision.

The cloud and fire also embodied the multifaceted nature of God's relationship with his people. The cloud symbolized his comforting presence, a shelter from life's harsh realities. The fire symbolized his consuming passion, igniting their hearts with zeal and purpose. Together, these manifestations encapsulated the depth of God's care and provision, assuring the Israelites—and us today—that no matter how desolate the wilderness may seem, his guiding hand is ever-present, leading us toward the promised destination of his divine purpose.

7. Why did God lead the Israelites on the "long route" toward the promised land? What did he understand about his people at this stage of their journey?

8. What did God reveal about his nature through the pillar of cloud and fire? Why did the Israelites need to know this about the one who was leading them?

REFLECT

Our hope, when navigating this life, is in this fact that God wins. His is the story of the entire Bible, and at the end of the story, he is the one who is still standing. Nothing has—or ever will—thwart his eternal purposes. Even though it may appear at times that the enemy is winning, the ultimate outcome is secure because God is faithful. He always does what he promises.

When Adam and Eve sinned against the Lord, it certainly appeared that Satan had won a decisive victory. The couple were forced to leave the presence of God and the Garden of Eden, and humanity's relationship with their creator was severed. Yet right there in the first story of sin, God provided hope that a day would come when he would make all things right again. He said to the enemy, "I will put enmity between you and the woman, and between your offspring and hers; he will crush your head, and you will strike his heel" (Genesis 3:15).

God promised that a Savior would come who would crush the enemy and the sin that had entered into the world. He would defeat Satan and sin. This is exactly what Paul says that Jesus accomplished through his death and resurrection:

> [20] *But Christ has indeed been raised from the dead, the firstfruits of those who have fallen asleep.* [21] *For since death came through a man, the resurrection of the dead comes also through a man.* [22] *For as in Adam all die, so in Christ all will be made alive.* [23] *But each in turn: Christ, the firstfruits; then, when he comes, those who belong to him.* [24] *Then the end will come, when he hands over the kingdom to God the Father after he has destroyed all dominion, authority and power.* [25] *For he must reign until he has put all his enemies under his feet.* [26] *The last enemy to be destroyed is death.* [27] *For he "has put everything under his feet." Now when it says that "everything" has been put under him, it is clear that this does not include God himself, who put everything under Christ.* [28] *When he has done this, then the Son himself will be made subject to him who put everything under him, so that God may be all in all.*
>
> 1 Corinthians 15:20–28

Jesus proved that Satan, sin, and death would not have the final word. His empty tomb reveals that he was victorious over all three. After his resurrection, "God exalted him to the highest place and gave him the name that is above every name, that at the name of Jesus every knee should bow, in heaven and on earth and under the earth, and every tongue acknowledge that Jesus Christ is Lord, to the glory of God the Father" (Philippians 2:9-11). This is the victorious Christ we meet in the book of Revelation. He is seated on his rightful throne, ruling and reigning over the world after having defeated Satan, sin, and death.

Jesus' victory means that we can have hope regardless of what we face in life. This is the point Jesus made shortly before his death when he told his disciples, "In this world you will have trouble. But take heart! I have overcome the world" (John 16:33). The disciples needed this message. They would soon face the same type of persecution that Jesus had faced. Many would be killed for their faith. Jesus assured them that nothing on earth—not even death—was ultimate. He had overcome death and prepared an eternal home for them (see John 14:2–3).

9. How does the victory of Jesus over Satan, sin, and death impact your understanding of hope in the midst of all the challenges you face each day?

10. When you consider Jesus' assurance that he has overcome the world, how does that truth empower you to face trials and difficulties in your own life?

CLOSE

The apostle Paul, reflecting on what Christ had accomplished at the cross, posed this question: "Where, O death, is your victory? Where, O death, is your sting?" (1 Corinthians 15:55). For followers of Jesus, death is like a wasp without a stinger—a minor nuisance at best. It cannot do anything to harm us, so we can just swat it away. As Jesus said of us, "I give them eternal life, and they will never perish; no one will snatch them out of my hand" (John 10:28). Furthermore, we can know that nothing "will be able to separate us from the love of God" (Romans 8:39). So the worst that life has to offer (death) can do nothing to hurt us. We are his forever.

Paul concludes, "Therefore, my dear brothers and sisters, stand firm. Let nothing move you. Always give yourselves fully to the work of the Lord, because you know that your labor in the Lord is not in vain" (1 Corinthians 15:58). Firm. Immoveable. Always abounding in the work of the Lord. This is the life of someone who knows that God wins and, therefore, fears nothing.

In a football game, when a quarterback drops back to make a pass, the opposing players try to take him out. Sometimes the pocket around him collapses, and the quarterback gets rattled. The commentator might say that he has "happy feet," which means he has started running for his life rather than waiting for one of his receivers to break open. Effective quarterbacks don't get "happy feet." They trust their blockers and allow the receivers to run their routes. They are firm. Immoveable. Always abounding in the work of being a quarterback.

As Christians, we often get "happy feet." We sense that the world around us is collapsing and look for an escape. But God calls us to stand firm and trust in him—just like the effective quarterback trusts in his offensive line. Sure, the opponent seems scary as he crashes in around us, but there is really nothing to fear. As Paul wrote, "We are more than conquerors through him who loved us" (Romans 8:37). Our God is victorious, and he has made us into conquerors. We can persevere through anything—even life in a really messed up world.

11. How do you respond to the idea that death is like a wasp without a stinger? How should that truth inform the way you live as a disciple of Jesus?

12. What are some situations that have given you "happy feet"? How could you approach those situations with the mindset that you are a conqueror in Christ?

Lesson Two

LIVING IN LIGHT OF ETERNITY

Wealth is worthless in the day of wrath,
but righteousness delivers from death.

PROVERBS 11:4

"Do not store up for yourselves treasures
on earth, where moth and vermin destroy, and where
thieves break in and steal. But store up for
yourselves treasures in heaven."

MATTHEW 6:19–20

What is seen

is temporary,

but what is unseen

is eternal.

2 CORINTHIANS 4:18

WELCOME

"What you focus on is what you become." Psychologists often cite this phrase to encourage their clients to change their mindset on life. They know that when people focus on the positive, they are more likely to feel positive, and thus be motivated to go out and do positive things. This same idea is found in Scripture: "Above all else, guard your heart, for everything you do flows from it" (Proverbs 4:23). What is in your "heart" will direct your actions.

What is the focus of your life? Or, maybe more appropriately, what are you modeling your life after? I am so grateful to have mentors in my life—people who have encouraged me and who have set a good example for me to follow. My dad was my first mentor, and he is still a mentor to this day. I have business mentors, ministry mentors, athletic mentors, spiritual mentors, and mentors in other areas of my life. All of these individuals have helped shape me into the man I am today.

Right now, I have a mentor who is teaching me how to fly an airplane. I began a few years back when I received a gift of flight lessons. It was a passion that captured my heart from the start. Now, before you get the idea that I am soaring through the skies in a luxury private jet, know that my current reality is the humble confines of a 1960s model single-engine plane. Also, my flight instructor is almost half my age. Regardless, with his knowledge and experience, he has become my trusted mentor in the skies. He serves as a coach, guiding me through the intricacies of flight toward destinations that I once only dreamed of reaching.

My instructor's expertise and passion for flying have bridged any perceived divide that might exist because of our difference in age. In each lesson, he imparts to me not only technical skills but also a deeper understanding of the art and science of aviation. His guidance goes beyond mere instruction—it is a journey of shared experiences, challenges, and triumphs. As he leads me through the skies, I am reminded that true mentorship transcends age, as wisdom and passion intertwine to pave the way for dreams to take flight.

The authors of Scripture are our greatest mentors. Even though the age gap between us is vast—stretching back thousands of years—their timeless wisdom still offers guidance that shapes us and refines our focus and priorities. As we immerse ourselves in the writings of these ancient mentors, we discover profound truths that illuminate our understanding.

As we touched on in the previous lesson, the apostle John is one such mentor. In the book of Revelation, he gives us not only a picture of what will happen as we approach the end of days but also a picture of the new heaven and earth that will serve as our eternal home. As we meditate on the promises we find in Revelation, the text becomes more than just a prophetic revelation; it becomes a blueprint that enables us to navigate the complexities of life with confidence and purpose. It guides us toward the fulfillment of God's eternal purposes.

The question for us today is . . . are we focusing on these promises from God? Are we living our lives today in light of God's plans for us in eternity? Are we wholeheartedly agreeing with John when he writes, "Come, Lord Jesus" (Revelation 22:20) and keeping our eyes on him? Or is our focus locked in solely on what is in front of us in our day-to-day lives?

1. How would you answer these questions? Why do you think it is often so difficult to "set your [mind] on things above, not on earthly things" (Colossians 3:2)?

2. Who have been some of the greatest mentors in your life? What are the characteristics they displayed that made them so great?

READ

Don't Get Distracted

It is likely that you already have most of what you will be doing next week mapped out. There are certain job responsibilities that you have to perform. Meetings you must attend. Household projects you need to complete. And there are responsibilities related to your relationships. If you are married or have a family, there is a wide array of tasks that are required for you to perform to care for those you love. Even if you don't have a spouse or children, you have relationships with friends and family that require your attention.

The world of technology has expedited the pace of life and, in many ways, has made our lives better and easier. In the days before cell phones, people had to rely on printed maps for guidance. Getting lost was a routine aspect of life. But now, we can get turn-by-turn driving directions dictated to us through the GPS on our phones. We can be reached at all times by family members if there is a crisis. Apps have also made our lives easier in many ways.

Yet, this can be a double-edged sword. The downside to technology—as we know only too well—is that we are always accessible to others. The incessant ping on our phones continuously reminds us there is someone who needs or wants our time. There is a great temptation to constantly check our screens for the latest text or update on social media. Apps can be helpful . . . but they can also keep us from doing things that we know are of greater priority. We are an incredibly distracted generation with little time for rest.

In the midst of the allure of these distractions, the teachings of Jesus resonate with profound relevance and challenge. In one passage, he compels all who are weary and burdened to come to him, and he will give them rest (see Matthew 11:28). In another teaching, he challenges his followers to consider their priorities:

> [19] *"Do not store up for yourselves treasures on earth, where moths and vermin destroy, and where thieves break in and steal.* [20] *But store up for yourselves treasures in heaven, where moths and vermin do not destroy, and where thieves do not break in and steal.* [21] *For where your treasure is, there your heart will be also.*
>
> [22] *"The eye is the lamp of the body. If your eyes are healthy, your whole body will be full of light.* [23] *But if your eyes are unhealthy, your whole body will be full of darkness. If then the light within you is darkness, how great is that darkness!*
>
> [24] *"No one can serve two masters. Either you will hate the one and love the other, or you will be devoted to the one and despise the other. You cannot serve both God and money.*
>
> Matthew 6:19–24

In this passage, Jesus addresses the human tendency to prioritize earthly possessions, which are susceptible to decay and theft, over the eternal treasures of heaven. His words serve as a poignant reminder that the pursuit of material wealth can create a conflict of allegiance, as one cannot serve "both God and money" simultaneously. For this reason, Jesus urges his followers to release their tight grasp on earthly treasures and redirect their focus and devotion toward God and the enduring treasures of the heavenly realm.

3. What are some of the dangers of not keeping your focus on Christ?

4. What does it mean that "where your treasure is, there your heart will be also"?

Pursue Heavenly Treasures

Notice that Jesus doesn't provide any information about the value of these heavenly treasures. While we are certainly familiar with the worth of earthly treasures, it is much harder for us to put a price on the treasures that God is storing up for us in a place where we are not currently residing. So what can we surmise about the worth of these heavenly treasures?

In another teaching, Jesus said, "The kingdom of heaven is like treasure hidden in a field. When a man found it, he hid it again, and then in his joy went and sold all he had and bought that field" (Matthew 13:44). Jesus continued, "The kingdom of heaven is like a merchant looking for fine pearls. When he found one of great value, he went away and sold everything he had and bought it" (verses 45–46). Clearly, the treasures of God's kingdom are of great worth—enough for the people in these parables to give up all they had to possess them.

This idea of giving up earthly possessions to gain heavenly treasure leads to another important point. Remember that Jesus told his listeners, "No one can serve two masters" (6:24). This means that we must actively renounce a selfish pursuit of worldly trinkets. Paul put it this way: " Command those who are rich in this present world not to be arrogant nor to put their hope in wealth, which is so uncertain. . . . Command them to do good, to be rich in good deeds, and to be generous and willing to share. In this way they will lay up treasure for themselves as a firm foundation for the coming age" (1 Timothy 6:17–19).

This is not to say that it is impossible for a wealthy man or woman to prioritize God's kingdom. There are certainly those who have been blessed with extraordinary wealth who have leveraged their earthly privilege to do much good for the kingdom of God. However, there are very real warnings in the Bible about having an infatuation with stuff. We find one such warning in the following encounter that Jesus had one day with a rich young ruler:

> [18] *A certain ruler asked him, "Good teacher, what must I do to inherit eternal life?"*
>
> [19] *"Why do you call me good?" Jesus answered. "No one is good—except God alone.* [20] *You know the commandments: 'You shall not commit adultery, you shall not murder, you shall not steal, you shall not give false testimony, honor your father and mother.'"*
>
> [21] *"All these I have kept since I was a boy," he said.*
>
> [22] *When Jesus heard this, he said to him, "You still lack one thing. Sell everything you have and give to the poor, and you will have treasure in heaven. Then come, follow me."*
>
> [23] *When he heard this, he became very sad, because he was very wealthy.* [24] *Jesus looked at him and said, "How hard it is for the rich to enter the kingdom of God!* [25] *Indeed, it is easier for a camel to go through the eye of a needle than for someone who is rich to enter the kingdom of God."*
>
> [26] *Those who heard this asked, "Who then can be saved?"*
>
> [27] *Jesus replied, "What is impossible with man is possible with God."*
>
> [28] *Peter said to him, "We have left all we had to follow you!"*
>
> [29] *"Truly I tell you," Jesus said to them, "no one who has left home or wife or brothers or sisters or parents or children for the sake of the kingdom of God* [30] *will fail to receive many times as much in this age, and in the age to come eternal life."*
>
> Luke 18:18–30

5. The rich young ruler wanted the eternal treasures of God. Why do you think it was so difficult for him to consider giving up his earthly treasures to obtain that eternal reward?

6. How were Peter and the disciples different from the rich young ruler? What did Jesus say would be their reward for focusing on the things of heaven?

Focus on God's Kingdom

King Solomon, the author of many of the proverbs in the Bible, was given a "wise and discerning heart" by the Lord (1 Kings 3:12). This wisdom led him to illuminate certain principles about righteousness and integrity—what we might consider "heavenly treasures." In the following proverb, among the myriad topics that Solomon explores, he highlights God's disdain for dishonesty, particularly in matters of commerce and trade:

> ¹ *The LORD detests dishonest scales,*
> *but accurate weights find favor with him.*
> ² *When pride comes, then comes disgrace,*
> *but with humility comes wisdom.*

³ *The integrity of the upright guides them,*
   but the unfaithful are destroyed by their duplicity.
⁴ *Wealth is worthless in the day of wrath,*
   but righteousness delivers from death. . . .
²⁵ *A generous person will prosper;*
   whoever refreshes others will be refreshed.
²⁶ *People curse the one who hoards grain,*
   but they pray God's blessing on the one who is willing to sell. . . .
²⁸ *Those who trust in their riches will fall,*
   but the righteous will thrive like a green leaf.

Proverbs 11:1–4, 25–26, 28

Solomon invites us to reflect on the significance of honesty and integrity in our daily lives and recognize that righteousness is the foundation of true prosperity and blessing from the Lord. This principle underscores the importance of fairness and honesty in all our dealings and emphasizes that true success and prosperity come from godly character.

Ultimately, "wealth is worthless" and "those who trust in their riches will fall." However, "a generous person will prosper" and "the righteous will thrive like a green leaf." In the end, there are only going to be a few things that matter. Wealth and the accumulation of material possessions are not going to be one of those things. What will matter is how we stewarded the resources and influence that we possessed.

Living in light of eternity means keeping our focus on the things of God's kingdom. In the words of Paul, "For now we see only a reflection as in a mirror; then we shall see face to face. Now I know in part; then I shall know fully, even as I am fully known" (1 Corinthians 13:12). This world is temporary and fleeting. All the wealth that we obtain here, "where moths and vermin destroy" (Matthew 6:19), will one day pass away and be worthless.

For this reason, we are to "not love the world or anything in the world" (1 John 2:15). Instead, we are to pursue the things of heaven, which will last into eternity, when we see God face to face—treasures such as "righteousness, godliness, faith, love, endurance and gentleness" (1 Timothy 6:11).

7. There are roughly 2,000 verses in the Bible that refer in some way to money and possessions. Why do you think this is such an important topic in Scripture?

8. Why is often difficult for those who have wealth to put their full trust in God?

REFLECT

As we embark on pursuing God's kingdom, two fundamental ideas emerge. First, we are called to pursue the God of the kingdom. We are to direct our hearts and minds toward an intimate relationship with him. This involves seeking God's presence, character, and will—cultivating a personal connection with the very source of the kingdom's power and authority.

As we go through our lives here on earth, we often lose sight of the fact that the greatest treasure in heaven is simply that God is there. We get to be with him! As John wrote, "God's dwelling place is now among the people, and he will dwell with them. They will be his people, and God himself will be with them and be their God" (Revelation 21:3). God will dwell with us in heaven, just as he did with Adam and Eve at the dawn of creation.

Remember that the Lord was physically present with them, walking in the garden in the cool of the day. Sin ruined that beautiful reality and led to a separation between God and humanity, but as we have seen throughout this series, the Lord continued to pursue people. He dwelt with the nation of Israel in the tabernacle and then in the temple in Jerusalem. Ultimately, God sent Jesus to dwell among people. He was God in the flesh—the exact image of God living among sinful humanity. Now, finally, at the end of time, with sin and death defeated, God is able to fully dwell with His people. We will know him without the separation of sin.

Those of us who are actively preparing for that day in the future should pursue intimacy with God in the present. We should seek to know him, love him, and dwell with him. After all, this is what we will be doing for all eternity—so why not start now? Of course, there is a tension in this, because we cannot perfectly and fully experience God's presence here on earth. We see "only a reflection" of eternity right now (1 Corinthians 13:12). We are already reconciled to God, and Satan, sin, and death have already been defeated. But we have not yet seen God fully. Satan, sin, and death still exist, and we still grapple with them. Life is already but not yet.

Caught in this tension, disciples of Jesus are meant to live in light of what is to come. One way they do this is by living in expectation of his coming. Jesus described it like a bride on her wedding night (see Matthew 25:1–13). She is longing for the bridegroom to come. She can't sleep. Her thoughts are on the future that awaits. This is what God's people are to be like. We are to live with a longing for Jesus to return and take us to be with Him forever.

While this life brings pleasure and joy in seasons, we are meant to desire a better day—one in which we will live with God without stain of sin. As Paul wrote, "For in this hope we were saved. But hope that is seen is no hope at all. Who hopes for what they already have? But if we hope for what we do not yet have, we wait for it patiently" (Romans 8:24–25). We are meant to awaken each day with a longing for God to finally save his people and fix this world.

This brings us a second fundamental idea: we are to establish and advance the kingdom of God on earth. This involves aligning our lives with the principles, values, and purposes of God's kingdom. We work toward its realization in our lives and in the world around us. Jesus made this point when he encouraged us to not be anxious—particularly about what we are to eat or what we will wear. God, our Father, knows that we need these things and will surely give them to us, just as he does to the lilies of the field and the birds of the air. Instead of worrying about these things, we are to seek first the kingdom of God (see Matthew 6:33).

To seek God's kingdom means to pursue the things the king cares about. A human king knows his subjects care about his kingdom because they are willing to go to battle to defend the rights, freedoms, and possessions of the kingdom. In a similar way, God, as the heavenly king, expects his people to go to battle on his behalf—except that we are not fighting a physical army, nor are we fighting human opponents. Paul reminds us that "our struggle is not against flesh and blood" but against "the spiritual forces of evil" (Ephesians 6:12).

Our calling is clear. We are to declare and demonstrate God's mission to save sinners and fix the world through Jesus Christ. As we invest in that work, we fight for what our king cares about. We make this world a bit more like heaven and seek to find people who we can add into that kingdom. This is the work of those who prioritize the kingdom of God.

9. What steps are you taking to pursue your relationship with God in the present?

10. What steps are you taking to establish and advance God's kingdom on earth?

CLOSE

As we pursue God's kingdom, we are also to seek "his righteousness" (Matthew 6:33). This means conforming our lives to his holy standard of living. God promises that he will ultimately rid us of sin so we can abound in the characteristics that are indicative of his holiness (see Romans 8:28–30). We will be without sin one day! But until that day, we are to seek to eradicate sin from our lives and embody the fruit of God's Spirit (see Galatians 5:22–23). We invest in those qualities that will exist in heaven and eternity.

This work is a fight. Paul calls us to put sin to death (see Romans 8:12–13). We don't play games with it—we kill it. We put on "the full armor God" (Ephesians 6:11) and remain "alert and of sober mind" (1 Peter 5:8) to the enemy's schemes. Peter's words call to mind a clearheaded readiness. We are to be on our toes, awake and alert, knowing we can be attacked at any moment. It is similar to the type of driving you should do if you are in a torrential downpour. When it's sunny outside, you can set the car on cruise control and let your mind drift. But when the rain starts beating against the window, you slow down, grip the steering wheel, turn off the radio, and watch the road. Storms call for intense focus.

This is the way God's people are meant to move through life. The storms are raging. It's a dark and scary world. Of course, we know that one day the sun will break through and we will be with God. In fact, John pictures the new heaven and earth without a sun—not because it will be dark there but because Jesus' presence will light up everything with his glory (see Revelation 21:23). In the meantime, we are to be sober and alert as we endure the storms of this world, looking forward to the day when the clouds part and the true "Sun" shines forever.

11. What are some practical ways that you seek God's righteousness in your life?

12. What does it mean for you to engage in battle against sin every day?

Lesson Three

THE WAY IS NARROW

"Though the mountains be shaken and the hills be removed, yet my unfailing love for you will not be shaken nor my covenant of peace be removed."

ISAIAH 54:10

"I am the way and the truth and the life. No one comes to the Father except through me."

JOHN 14:6

"Whoever believes in the Son has eternal life, but whoever rejects the Son will not see life."

JOHN 3:36

WELCOME

Several years ago, our family went on a trip to see some amazing National Parks. We had recently purchased a very used RV from a youth pastor, and for its maiden voyage we decided to embark on a 5,000-mile trip from Atlanta and back. Everything was going great until we got to an extremely rural part of southern Colorado along the border of New Mexico.

I had been using an app on my phone for directions, and it had not led me astray . . . yet. But the further we drove, the paved road turned into a gravel road. We began to encounter a steep incline, and the road grew narrower and narrower. Out of my driver's side window, I could see the drop-off over the ledge getting deeper and deeper. Then we came to a bridge.

I stopped and stepped out of the RV so that I could assess the situation. The bridge had a steel support structure, but the roadbed was made of wooden planks. There was no room to turn around. Backing down the mountain was also not an option, because, did I mention, we were towing a car behind us. I realized that my only option was to go across the bridge.

I assessed the structure again. It seemed sound enough. So I got back in the driver's seat, put the RV in drive, and gunned it. Ten seconds later, we were safely on the other side. Sometimes, there is only one way that you can get to your destination!

Jesus made a startling proclamation near the end of the Sermon on the Mount: "Wide is the gate and broad is the road that leads to destruction, and many enter through it. But small is the gate and narrow the road that leads to life, and only a few find it" (Matthew 7:13–14).

The image that Jesus presents is of that narrow mountain road. The way forward is difficult and can seem uncertain at times. This is why few opt to take it, preferring instead to stay on the wider freeways in the valley below. But Jesus knows those broader roads will not take us to our eternal destination. In fact, there is only one road that will get us there—and it is found by following the path that he sets for our lives. As he says to us, "I am the way and the truth and the life. No one comes to the Father except through me" (John 14:6).

In today's world, people often claim that there are many different roads to heaven. What is important, they say, is to live the most moral life you can—and not hurt anyone in the process. However, Jesus does not say that he is "a way" but "the way" to truth and life. No one comes to the Father—and experiences eternal life with him—except through Christ.

1. What are some of the messages you have heard from people in this world about the different ways that a person can realize eternal life?

2. What makes the idea of Jesus being the only way so difficult in our modern culture?

READ

Choose the Narrow Way to Life

So, what can we know about this one way that leads to eternal life? In Matthew 7:13–14, Jesus twice says this way is "narrow." In the original Greek, two different words are used in the passage for "narrow." In verse 13, the term is *stenēs*, which means physically pressed together or cramped. In verse 14, the term is *tethlimmenē*, which comes from the Greek root word *thlipsis*, meaning "tribulation." Forms of this word are generally translated as "persecuted" (as in 1 Thessalonians 3:4) and "pressed" (as in 2 Corinthians 4:8).

The way to eternal life is thus "narrow" because it is a path of opposition. It is not a road that everyone is willing to travel—and, for that reason, "only a few find it." Of course, this is not to say the road is closed to anyone. Jesus actually begins this section of his Sermon on the Mount with an open invitation to the journey: "Ask and it will be given to you; seek and you will find; knock and the door will be opened to you. For everyone who asks receives; the one who seeks finds; and to the one who knocks, the door will be opened" (Matthew 7:7–8).

Rather, what Jesus is saying is that taking this road requires more than just talking about godly things or doing religious things. It involves more than just professing a belief in him. Jesus warns that some people who think they know him and say they follow him will actually be surprised to find out they are not really part of his group. They believe they are on the right path, but in truth they are going the wrong way. Only those who take the hard road of building their lives on the foundation of Christ and doing what he says will see heaven:

> [21] *"Not everyone who says to me, 'Lord, Lord,' will enter the kingdom of heaven, but only the one who does the will of my Father who is in heaven.* [22] *Many will say to me on that day, 'Lord, Lord, did we not prophesy in your name and in your name drive out demons and in your name perform many miracles?'* [23] *Then I will tell them plainly, 'I never knew you. Away from me, you evildoers!'*
>
> [24] *"Therefore everyone who hears these words of mine and puts them into practice is like a wise man who built his house on the rock.* [25] *The rain came down, the streams rose, and the winds blew and beat against that house; yet*

it did not fall, because it had its foundation on the rock. [26] *But everyone who hears these words of mine and does not put them into practice is like a foolish man who built his house on sand.* [27] *The rain came down, the streams rose, and the winds blew and beat against that house, and it fell with a great crash."*

Matthew 7:21–27

Jesus states that being his follower is like building a house on a strong foundation instead of shaky ground. Even though it might be hard sometimes to follow what he says—like drilling into solid rock—it is worth it because it leads to eternal life. When we make Jesus the foundation of our lives, and build our lives on what God says is right, we can be secure about what our final destination will be. We take part in Jesus' promise, "I give them eternal life, and they shall never perish; no one will snatch them out of my hand" (John 10:28).

3. How do you respond to Jesus' statement that there will be those who call him "Lord," and even do works in his name, who will not enter the kingdom of heaven?

4. What are some things you have to give up in order to pursue the narrow way?

Avoid the Broad Path to Destruction

Those who build their lives on Christ and take his narrow way will experience eternal life. But the same is not true of those who build their lives on any other foundation. Those who take the broad way—the easy route—will find that it "leads to destruction." Jesus says this will be a place marked by "weeping and gnashing of teeth" (Matthew 13:42). Sadness and regret are all these individuals will experience for eternity. Their fate will be sealed in the end because of their continual rejection of Jesus throughout their lives.

For the truth is that those whose end is destruction get there because they choose the things of this world over the things of God. They do not want the Lord to be a part of their story . . . and he ultimately grants their request. They discover that "the wages of sin is death," while for followers of Christ, "the gift of God is eternal life" (Romans 6:23). Paul makes the following statement about those who make this tragic choice to reject God:

> 18 The wrath of God is being revealed from heaven against all the godlessness and wickedness of people, who suppress the truth by their wickedness, 19 since what may be known about God is plain to them, because God has made it plain to them. 20 For since the creation of the world God's invisible qualities—his eternal power and divine nature—have been clearly seen, being understood from what has been made, so that people are without excuse.
>
> 21 For although they knew God, they neither glorified him as God nor gave thanks to him, but their thinking became futile and their foolish hearts were darkened. 22 Although they claimed to be wise, they became fools 23 and exchanged the glory of the immortal God for images made to look like a mortal human being and birds and animals and reptiles.
>
> 24 Therefore God gave them over in the sinful desires of their hearts to sexual impurity for the degrading of their bodies with one another. 25 They exchanged the truth about God for a lie, and worshiped and served created things rather than the Creator—who is forever praised. Amen.
>
> Romans 1:18–25

There are a few important points to consider in this passage. First, Paul notes that "since the creation of the world God's invisible qualities—his eternal power and divine nature—have been clearly seen" to all people. The world in which we live is certainly messed up. People do all sorts of evil things. Tragedies strike with no advanced warning. However, this does not mean that things are as bad as they could be. In reality, things could be much worse.

In this life, we all have moments of joy. We experience beauty, pleasure, happiness, companionship, and love. Each of these are gifts from God, even though people in this world might not acknowledge them as such. There are also countless ways that God is caring for individuals each and every day of their lives. He shows his kindness to them and gives them evidence of his character. He protects them from harm and preserves their lives. This is true for all people, not just for those who know Christ. God's grace is ever-present.

Paul states that these acts of God's mercy are meant to have a certain impact on people. It should first lead them to a place of repentance, where they glorify "him as God" and give "thanks to him." As Paul later writes, "Do you show contempt for the riches of his kindness, forbearance and patience, not realizing that God's kindness is intended to lead you to repentance?" (Romans 2:4). God's kindness is intended to lead people to repentance.

There is an interesting example of this found in the story of the Israelites after they had been freed from Egypt. God had led them by a pillar of cloud by day and a pillar of fire by night. He had delivered them from the Egyptian army that pursued them. He had demonstrated many mercies to them. But now that they were in the wilderness, they were hungry and weary. So they cried out to Moses and Aaron, "If only we had died by the Lord's hand in Egypt! There we sat around pots of meat and ate all the food we wanted, but you have brought us out into this desert to starve this entire assembly to death" (Exodus 16:3).

In their frustration, the people longed for the familiarity of their past. They recalled all the food they had in Egypt . . . even though they had been in slavery there. Yet God's kindness to them shone through even in the midst of their discontent. Instead of abandoning them or punishing their ungratefulness, the Lord responded with compassion and generosity. He provided manna from heaven, sustaining them with nourishment in the midst of the desert.

This act exemplifies the unwavering kindness of God, who extends his grace even when met with complaints and ingratitude. It serves as a poignant reminder of God's steadfast love and provision even in our moments of doubt and dissatisfaction. But these acts of kindness are intended to provoke repentance. God's desire for the Israelites was for them to turn away from their grumbling and put their faith in him. He wanted them to avoid the path to destruction.

5. How do you define repentance? What does it look like in your life?

6. How have God's acts of kindness toward you brought about repentance?

Recognize God's Patience and Kindness

God loves people and gives them space to turn away from their sin—to choose the path to eternal life rather than the road to destruction. As Peter writes, "The Lord is not slow in keeping his promise, as some understand slowness. Instead he is patient with you, not wanting anyone to perish, but everyone to come to repentance" (2 Peter 3:9).

A few tangible examples here might help. Some people consistently cave to the lure of addictive behavior. Time and time again, they seem to escape by the skin of their teeth, emerging from risky situations without harm. Other people bounce from one relationship to the next, giving of themselves to each potential suitor. Each failed relationship ends with them wondering why they cannot find lasting love—but it is clear that things could have gone much worse. In each situation, the Lord demonstrated his patience and kindness.

The question is how these friends will respond to that kindness. Perhaps they will assume they have gotten away with their sin and continue in the same destructive patterns of behavior. This would be showing "contempt for the riches of [God's] kindness," to use Paul's words. Your friends would continue down the wide road that leads to destruction.

Or perhaps these friends will allow their failures to awaken their souls and lead them to understand their need for God. They will begin to contemplate just how merciful God has been to spare them from the full extent of their evil—and turn back to God before it is too late. This would be "realizing that God's kindness is intended to lead [them] to repentance," to again use Paul's words. Your friends would choose to go down a new path that leads to life in Christ. The prophet Isaiah beautifully encapsulates this eternal nature of God's kindness and faithfulness when he writes:

> *"Though the mountains be shaken*
> *and the hills be removed,*
> *yet my unfailing love for you will not be shaken*
> *nor my covenant of peace be removed,"*
> *says the Lord, who has compassion on you.*

Isaiah 54:10

This profound declaration illustrates the steadfastness of God's love, which transcends the temporal and earthly. It speaks to the enduring nature of his compassion, even in the midst of the turmoil and uncertainties of life. Like a rock among shifting sands, God's kindness remains constant, offering solace and assurance to those who seek refuge in him. God's words through Isaiah serve as a poignant reminder of the unchanging character of our Lord and his boundless love for humanity—a love that knows no end and extends throughout eternity.

7. Think of a situation in which the Lord was kind to you in spite of your actions or behavior. How did you respond to his kindness?

8. What are some practical ways that you have experienced God's patience in your life?

REFLECT

We find evidence of God's patience throughout the pages of Scripture. In the Old Testament, we see him not only being patient with the Israelites but also with foreign nations like Assyria, sending prophets like Jonah to warn them of their impending destruction if they did not repent (see Jonah 4:4). In the New Testament, we see God giving sinners like Paul time to repent from sin and place their faith in Jesus (see Acts 9:5). We still see God being patient today. He is extending his grace to people at this very moment by giving them time to repent.

However, there will come a time when this opportunity to repent will end. Paul, after stating that God's kindness is intended to lead people to repentance, adds, "But because of your stubbornness and your unrepentant heart, you are storing up wrath against yourself for the day of God's wrath, when his righteous judgment will be revealed" (Romans 2:5).

The image that Paul presents of "God's wrath" is like a dam storing up water. It builds and builds until the day it is released, at which point all the water bursts forth at once. A day is coming when God's wrath will be poured out on those who persist in their sin and rebellion. Paul uses similar language in Ephesians 2:3 when he says that those who are dead in their trespasses are deserving of God's wrath. We typically speak of people as children of God, but Paul argues that those without faith in Jesus are children of his wrath.

Wrath isn't a characteristic we often use when we think of God. He is a God of love, right? Yet because of this love, he must also be a God of wrath. Wrath is only anti-God if it is unfair. If he were to whimsically lash out at people with no cause or warning, then that would be unfit for God. But God isn't unjust. His wrath is completely fair. He has consistently and clearly communicated who he is and what he desires. His law is clear. He has also told us that he will judge those who rebel against his law (see 1 Peter 4:3–5). We know what God expects and the consequences if we fail. God is entirely just to demonstrate his wrath to sinners.

The beautiful thing about God is that he is not just a God of wrath but also a God of mercy. He made a way for sinners to avoid his wrath by placing it on Jesus. This is what Jesus meant when he spoke of the cup that he would drink (see Matthew 26:39; Mark 14:36; Luke 22:42), with "cup" referring to the wrath of God (see Jeremiah 25:15). Jesus drank the cup of God's wrath that had been stored up against humanity. He consumed every last drop. Now, those who have faith in him and what he accomplished do not have to drink that wrath.

Perhaps you have heard people say that Christians are "saved." The word itself demands a question: Saved from what? If a swimmer is rescued in the middle of the lake, then we know that person was saved from drowning. A homeowner with a working fire alarm might be saved from a fire that would have destroyed the home. But from what is a Christian saved?

The answer is God's wrath. Yes, it is true that there are all sorts of other benefits that come from having faith in Jesus—hope, mission, friendships, and a host of other blessings that we receive from God. But first and foremost is the peace that comes from knowing our sins are forgiven and we will never, ever have to face the wrath of God. We are free. This is likely why Jesus referred to his way being easy and his yoke being light (see Matthew 11:28–30). There is true freedom found in knowing that we are no longer children of God's wrath.

9. How do you respond to this truth found in Scripture that God's wrath will one day be poured out against those who have remained in rebellion against him?

10. How would you describe what it means to be "saved" to someone who didn't know Christ? Who in your world needs to hear this message today?

CLOSE

The fate of your friends and loved ones who have not accepted Christ as their Savior is not yet sealed. Today could be the day of their salvation. Remember that those who will face God's wrath for eternity will do so because they made a choice. They will receive what they wanted in this life. You would think that no one would ever make this choice—but remember Jesus' parable of the two gates. The road to destruction is wide and filled with many travelers.

Those among us who have chosen the path to life have many reasons to praise God. We have received innumerable blessings from him. We have witnessed God's kindness produce genuine repentance in our lives. We have been given the right to be called children of God. We are walking the narrow path and, by the grace of God, will one day reach our destination.

11. What do you think makes the wide gate and broad road that leads to destruction so compelling to people? Why do so many choose to walk that path?

12. What reasons can you personally cite for praising God today?

Lesson Four

WE SHALL BE CHANGED

The life of mortals is like grass, they flourish like a flower of the field; the wind blows over it and it is gone, and its place remembers it no more.

PSALM 103:15–16

The world and its desires pass away, but whoever does the will of God lives forever.

1 JOHN 2:17

"Truly I tell you,
today you
will be with me
in paradise."

LUKE 23:43

WELCOME

Each January, millions of people around the world determine to make certain changes to their lives as part of a New Year's resolution. For some, those changes are related to exercise or diet. Others commit to making changes in the way they spend their time, or how much media they consume, or how much technology they use in a given week. Whatever the exact nature of the change, there is a sense in all of us that we would like for things to be different.

Change is a normal part of life. There are some forms of change that we can control—like those New Year's resolutions. But other types of change are outside our control. Our health suddenly changes. Our jobs morph over time. Our families move through various stages, with each transition bringing a new level of complexity. Unfortunately, much of the change we encounter moves in the negative direction.

Things devolve over time as we move through life. Our bodies are the greatest example of this. The older we get, the more our bodies show signs of wear and tear. The pickup ball game now means a few days of subsequent aches and pains. We can't jump as high or run as fast as we once did. Even activities that require zero work, like sleeping, can prove difficult as we age.

Recently, I was on a family trip, and my seventeen-year-old son wanted to go for a run. I used to be an avid runner in my thirties and early forties. We had a six-mile path by our house, and I ran it multiple times per week. But now I am in my late forties.

We set out, and of course I wanted to keep up with him and was determined to not let him outpace me. I was dying as we ran, but I kept pace. (I am sure he took it easy on me.) However, it was the days after the run that presented the most problems.

My knees swelled up. I had aches and pains. I had to resign myself to the fact that my best running days might be behind me.

Try as we might to fight it, our bodies will ultimately run down. This can seem like a morbid thought. We all know that we will die, sooner or later, but we try to block the thought out of our minds as much as we can. However, regardless of whether we want to face it or not, the reality is that every living creature on this earth is destined to one day experience death.

1. What types of changes are the most difficult for you to face?

2. What situations or circumstances prompt you to think about death?

READ

An Undeniable Reality

Death should not surprise anyone. Back in the Garden of Eden, we read how God judged humanity's sin with the punishment of physical death. He said to Adam and Eve, "Dust you are and to dust you will return" (Genesis 3:19). A few chapters later, in the list of Adam's descendants, we find evidence of this punishment as person after person is introduced into God's story with the concluding tag, "and then he died" (5:5, 8, 11, 14, 17, 20, 27, 31).

Everyone dies. The psalmist said it this way: "My days are like the evening shadow; I wither away like grass" (Psalm 102:11). Quite the uplifting thought! We are like a flimsy blade of grass that will one day wither away, without so much as a memory of our existence.

As stated previously, Solomon was one of the wisest people to ever live (see 1 Kings 4:31). He also had everything that a human being could ever want to have—wealth, riches, power, position, prestige. Yet he still had to deal with the fact that he would not live forever. A good portion of the book of Ecclesiastes, which he wrote, is Solomon dealing with the reality that his days on this earth would not last forever:

> ¹ *There is a time for everything,*
>   *and a season for every activity under the heavens:*
> ² *a time to be born and a time to die,*
>   *a time to plant and a time to uproot,*
> ³ *a time to kill and a time to heal,*
>   *a time to tear down and a time to build,*
> ⁴ *a time to weep and a time to laugh,*
>   *a time to mourn and a time to dance,*
> ⁵ *a time to scatter stones and a time to gather them,*
>   *a time to embrace and a time to refrain from embracing,*
> ⁶ *a time to search and a time to give up,*
>   *a time to keep and a time to throw away,*
> ⁷ *a time to tear and a time to mend,*
>   *time to be silent and a time to speak,*

⁸ a time to love and a time to hate,
*   a time for war and a time for peace.*

⁹ What do workers gain from their toil? ¹⁰ I have seen the burden God has
laid on the human race. ¹¹ He has made everything beautiful in its time. He
has also set eternity in the human heart; yet no one can fathom what God
has done from beginning to end.

Ecclesiastes 3:1–11

3.   What are some tangible ways that death has impacted your life on this earth?

4.   Solomon writes that there is a time for everything—including death. What does
he mean when he then says that God has set "eternity in the human heart"?

Life Is Like a Mist

Lula Bess, my wife's grandmother, was born in 1917. She lived through the Great Depression and multiple wars. She was married for more than sixty years, raised five children, and had many grandchildren and great-grandchildren. She passed away in 2018 at the age of 101.

Tanya, who was like an adopted daughter in our family, passed away in 2022 at the age of twenty-seven. Tanya was born in Cameroon. She was raised by missionaries after her mother and twin sister died in childbirth. They moved back to the United States when Tanya was five, and we met her when she was eighteen. Tanya came into our lives just as we were having our fourth child, and she was a huge help. She ended up meshing into our family and living in our basement apartment for more than five years. When she died from acute liver failure and other medical complications, it dealt a striking blow to us. It was like we had lost a child.

At the funeral for Lula Bess, it almost became cliché when people came up and said to us, "She lived to a ripe old age." At Tanya's funeral, we heard many people say, "She died way too young."

The question I pondered after both funerals was, *Compared to what?* When we say 101 is "a ripe old age," to what are we comparing it? When we say someone died too young, what are we using as a benchmark? Of course, what we are comparing is the life expectancy rate of humans. However, for believers, human life expectancy is not the correct metric. We have hope in an eternity with Jesus. Our lives are not measured in finite terms but in eternal ones. James poignantly captures this fleeting nature of human life in the following passage:

> [13] *Now listen, you who say, "Today or tomorrow we will go to this or that city, spend a year there, carry on business and make money."* [14] *Why, you do not even know what will happen tomorrow. What is your life? You are a mist that appears for a little while and then vanishes.* [15] *Instead, you ought to say, "If it is the Lord's will, we will live and do this or that."* [16] *As it is, you boast in your arrogant schemes. All such boasting is evil.* [17] *If anyone, then, knows the good they ought to do and doesn't do it, it is sin for them.*
>
> James 4:13–17

James states in this passage that our lives are like "a mist that appears for a little while." Indeed, for those residing in colder climates, the visual of breath dissipating into the air is a daily reminder of life's impermanence. The analogy vividly illustrates the brevity of our existence, highlighting how quickly moments come and go, leaving behind only memories. Just as the breath evaporates into the ether, so too does our time on this earth pass swiftly.

James offers a sobering reflection on the fragility of life and the importance of cherishing each moment, living with purpose, and making the most of the time we have been given. He invites us to ponder the transient nature of our lives and seek meaning beyond the temporal. This comes by placing our hope not in the things of this world but the things of God. We embrace a perspective that transcends the ephemeral and focuses on the eternal.

5. What point is James making about the plans that people make for the future when he states that human life is like a mist?

6. What does it mean to make plans for the future with "the Lord's will" in mind? What would that look like at a practical level in your life?

An Undeniable Hope

Many of us have witnessed the reality of death. We have seen it play out in the death of those we love deeply. Here one minute . . . and gone the next. Death is crushing.

The believers in Corinth were evidently feeling the sting of death in their community. They had many questions for Paul about what would happen when their time on earth was complete. They had heard from the apostle that there would be a resurrection of the dead. However, some were doubting it, while others were unsure of how it would take place.

Paul responded to their doubts and questions by first reminding them of the gospel that he had given to them. He stressed to them, "By this gospel you are saved, if you hold firmly to the word I preached to you" (1 Corinthians 15:2).

Paul then reminded them that Jesus had been "raised on the third day according to the Scriptures" (verse 4) and that he had appeared to a number of witnesses. Last of all, Christ had appeared to Paul himself.

Paul then comes to his main point: "If it is preached that Christ has been raised from the dead, how can some of you say that there is no resurrection of the dead? If there is no resurrection of the dead, then not even Christ has been raised. And if Christ has not been raised, our preaching is useless and so is your faith" (verses 12–14).

Paul is saying here that death for the Christian follows the pattern of Jesus. In fact, Jesus' resurrection was the "firstfruits" of what will happen to all of God's people (verse 20). The word *firstfruits* itself communicates the principle. When a farmer sees the firstfruits of the harvest in the spring, he knows that more is to come. The firstfruits of the harvest isn't the end; it's merely the beginning of what is to come. So, too, is the resurrection of Jesus.

Paul continues, "For as in Adam all die, so in Christ all will be made alive" (verse 22). This is a great connection. Adam's sin brought death to all those in his family line—hence, all people. But Jesus' resurrection brings life to all those in his family line—those who have been born again through their faith in him. Paul concludes this point in the following passage:

> **42** *So will it be with the resurrection of the dead. The body that is sown is perishable, it is raised imperishable;* **43** *it is sown in dishonor, it is raised in glory; it is sown in weakness, it is raised in power;* **44** *it is sown a natural body, it is raised a spiritual body.*
>
> *If there is a natural body, there is also a spiritual body.* **45** *So it is written: "The first man Adam became a living being"; the last Adam, a life-giving spirit.* **46** *The spiritual did not come first, but the natural, and after that the spiritual.* **47** *The first man was of the dust of the earth; the second man is of heaven.* **48** *As was the earthly man, so are those who are of the earth; and as is the heavenly man, so also are those who are of heaven.* **49** *And just as we have borne the image of the earthly man, so shall we bear the image of the heavenly man.*
>
> 1 Corinthians 15:42–49

Followers of Christ can place their hope in this promise that what happened to Jesus will one day happen to them. They can say, along with Paul, "Where, O death, is your victory? Where, O death, is your sting?" (verse 55).

For Christians, death means change—and a change for the better. For them, "to live is Christ and to die is gain" (Philippians 1:21). They understand that as they work to fulfill God's mission for them on earth, the change that is coming in eternity—and the rewards they will receive there—are better than anything they can imagine.

7. Why do you think Paul began his argument of what would happen to believers at the resurrection by first reminding them of Jesus' physical resurrection?

8. What key insights does Paul provide to the Corinthians about what the resurrection of their bodies will be like? How does this give you hope as you think about your death?

REFLECT

Followers of Jesus will "bear the image of the heavenly man" (1 Corinthians 15:49). What astounding news. The image of God we were given at creation will be fully restored. We will be without sin and, even better, we will no longer be able to sin. Our bodies will no longer decay and there will be no more fear of death. Relationships will be perfect and whole.

On that day, "'[God] will wipe every tear from their eyes. There will be no more death' or mourning or crying or pain, for the old order of things has passed away" (Revelation 21:4). As J.R.R. Tolkien says in *The Lord of the Rings*, "everything sad will come untrue." Imagine this for a moment. Everything that makes you cry will be gone—and not gone in the same way that pain is gone in your life now. Right now, even when things seem to be calm, there is always the nagging dread that it is only temporary. Something else bad is sure to happen soon. This is not the case in heaven. Evil and sin will be gone forever and it will be impossible for them to return.

Paul wrote to another group of believers in Thessalonica, in part, to encourage them with this truth. Much like the believers in Corinth, they were feeling the sting of death in their community. Their loved ones were dying, and they wanted to know how to respond. What should they do? How should they find hope? Paul responded by saying, "Brothers and sisters, we do not want you to be uninformed about those who sleep in death, so that you do not grieve like the rest of mankind, who have no hope" (1 Thessalonians 4:13). He then added:

> [16] *For the Lord himself will come down from heaven, with a loud command, with the voice of the archangel and with the trumpet call of God, and the dead in Christ will rise first.* [17] *After that, we who are still alive and are left will be caught up together with them in the clouds to meet the Lord in the air. And so we will be with the Lord forever.* [18] *Therefore encourage one another with these words.*
>
> 1 Thessalonians 4:16–18

What makes death frightening is the fear of the unknown. We find hope in things that are within the realm of our control, and death feels so out of control. This is why

God wants us to know enough about death and what is to come—so we can find encouragement and hope.

Paul goes so far as to write these remarkable words: "I consider that our present sufferings are not worth comparing with the glory that will be revealed in us" (Romans 8:18). What are these present sufferings? They are the atrocities of wars and evils of sex trafficking and human slavery. They are the effects of deplorable poverty, debilitating cancers, and every other blight on human existence that is currently present in this fallen world.

Paul says all these evils are not even worth comparing to what is to come. It's like a new mom who has just gone through the pains of labor. She looks back on the agony with a different perspective when she holds her beautiful new baby in her arms. The pain isn't even worth comparing to the supreme joy of being a mom! In the same way, "the whole creation has been groaning as in the pains of childbirth" (verse 22). We are dealing with the pain of the moment. But one day, we will look back on the pain of this life, and it will seem insignificant.

This is not meant to minimize the pain of this life. Evil is real and suffering is excruciating. The pain that we experience certainly does not feel light and momentary. But it will be!

9. What form are the "present sufferings" of the world taking in your life?

10. How could you view these sufferings like a mom going through the agony of giving birth—that the pain isn't worth comparing to the joy you will receive?

CLOSE

Paul writes in 1 Thessalonians 4:18 that we are to "encourage one another with these words." We are not to keep God's promise of eternal life to ourselves but are to share it with others. Imagine you are watching an intense thriller. Midway through the movie, your friends are freaking out about what is to come. But you're calm. Why? Because you have seen the movie before. You know how it is going to end. So you're not nearly as rattled as they are.

In same way, as a follower of Christ, you don't have to freak out about what is to come. Why? Because God has told you what will happen. He has given you the ultimate "spoiler" as to how everything will end. He now calls you to encourage others with that good news—reminding those who are suffering of the great joy that awaits all who are in Christ Jesus.

The hope that you possess is not only a source of personal strength but also a compelling witness to others. You are called to live in such a way that our hope stands out in stark contrast to the despair that is so prevalent in the world (see 1 Peter 3:15). This conspicuous hope prompts unbelievers to inquire about the source of your resolve, opening the door for you to have conversations with them about faith and salvation.

When you endure suffering with grace and trust in God, it becomes an opportunity for you to demonstrate the transformative power of Christ. Through your resilience in the face of trials, you can effectively communicate the peace that comes from a relationship with Jesus. By sharing your experiences and pointing others toward the source of your hope, you fulfill your mission to be an ambassador of Christ and invite others to discover the way to salvation.

11. Who is someone in your life who needs to receive this encouragement today? What steps could you take to begin sharing the hope you have found in Christ?

12. In what ways do you think people are seeing the hope you have in Jesus through the way you are living? What would need to change to make this more evident to others?

A SIGHT TO BEHOLD

"But now I have chosen Jerusalem for my Name to be there, and I have chosen David to rule my people Israel."

2 CHRONICLES 6:6

The city does not need the sun or the moon to shine on it, for the glory of God gives it light, and the Lamb is its lamp. The nations will walk by its light.

REVELATION 21:23–24

"Yet a time is coming . . .
when the true worshipers
will worship the Father in
the Spirit and in truth."

JOHN 4:23

WELCOME

When I was a kid, I went to Vacation Bible School in the summer. One of the high-lights for me was always craft time. During the week we would work on different crafts, usually to illustrate the Bible lessons. Then, on Friday night, our creations would be put on display for our parents and grandparents to see.

One particular year, the craft was to make something out of clay. I decided that I would make a clay bowl for my mom. I put my heart and soul into creating it. I shaped it, smoothed it, and formed it. I even talked to it—coercing and demanding the clay to move in the way that I wanted it to move. But when all was said and done, all I had was a clay lump. I don't know what it resembled, but it did not resemble a bowl. It might have passed as an ashtray, but it certainly did not resemble anything of beauty. My pottery skills were evident early on, and they were bad.

You have to wonder what Michelangelo was like as a kid growing up in the streets of Florence during the Italian Renaissance. Or what Mozart was like at the age of five, when he was already writing musical compositions and entertaining people with his talents at the piano. You can bet they both blew people away with their skill, even at such an early stage in their development. Certainly, their later work is proof of exceptional talent and innate skill far surpassing the average person. The truth is, you can tell a lot about someone from their creations.

The same is true about God. Paul writes that "what may be known about God is plain . . . because God has made it plain. For since the creation of the world God's invisible qualities—his eternal power and divine nature—have been clearly seen" (Romans 1:19-20). David states, "The heavens declare the glory of God; the skies proclaim the work of his hands" (Psalm 19:1). You can learn a great deal about God just by looking at his creation. You can see his skill and precision. You can see his sense of beauty and majesty. You can see his care for everything that he created—including us "lumps of clay" who were made in his own image (see Genesis 1:27).

1. What attributes of God are clear to you by looking at the world he made?

2. What does creation reveal to you about the character of God?

READ

A New Home

The first act of God's creation that we read about in Scripture was the formation of the universe and our world. As another psalmist wrote, "He set the earth on its foundations . . . covered it with the watery depths as with a garment" (Psalm 104:5–6). But this is not the only act of creation that we find in the Bible. God has been making something else for a very long time.

When Jesus was preparing his disciples for his imminent arrest and crucifixion, he said to them, "My Father's house has many rooms; if that were not so, would I have told you that I am going there to prepare a place for you? And if I go and prepare a place for you, I will come back and take you to be with me that you also may be where I am" (John 14:2–3).

This illustration of a home under construction would have been familiar to the disciples. Most homes in the ancient Near East were permanently under construction, as families would make room for additional family members through marriage and childbearing by simply adding on to their existing houses. The unfinished upper story of homes that can be found throughout the region to this day testifies to the fact that this practice of making rooms is still normative.

Jesus said that God is building on to his heavenly house in a similar manner. Each day, new members are being added to his family through spiritual adoption (see Ephesians 1:5). As this happens, new "rooms" are being added to the abode to make space for them.

What will this heavenly home be like? Well, remember that God made all of creation in the span of six days. In the 2,000 years since Jesus told his disciples about their heavenly home, he has been working to build that home for his people. The God who crafted Everest isn't going to build a shack for his family members in heaven (or a VBS clay bowl). Our heavenly home is sure to be the kind of place that will make the best this world has to offer pale in comparison.

We receive a glimpse of how amazing that home will be in the following passage:

> *⁹ One of the seven angels who had the seven bowls full of the seven last plagues came and said to me, "Come, I will show you the bride, the wife of the Lamb." ¹⁰ And he carried me away in the Spirit to a mountain great and high, and showed me the Holy City, Jerusalem, coming down out of heaven from God. ¹¹ It shone with the glory of God, and its brilliance was like that of a very precious jewel, like a jasper, clear as crystal. . . .*
>
> *²¹ The twelve gates were twelve pearls, each gate made of a single pearl. The great street of the city was of gold, as pure as transparent glass.*

*²² I did not see a temple in the city, because the Lord God Almighty and
the Lamb are its temple. ²³ The city does not need the sun or the moon to shine
on it, for the glory of God gives it light, and the Lamb is its lamp.*

Revelation 21:9–11, 21–23

3. How does it comfort you to know that God has a "room" that he has created
for you in his heavenly home?

4. What does the fact that God is continually "adding on" rooms say about his
nature? What does this say about his desire for all people to find salvation?

A New City

John reveals in his vision that our new heavenly home will be in a city: "I saw the
Holy City, the new Jerusalem, coming down out of heaven from God, prepared as a
bride beautifully dressed for her husband" (Revelation 21:2). Modern cities are fas-
cinating combinations of evil and beauty. Most are like Sodom and Gomorrah in the

days of Abraham, about which was said, "[they] gave themselves up to sexual immorality and perversion" (Jude 1:7).

However, the new Jerusalem that John sees is a "Holy City." It is a place without the stain of sin. In this city, there will be no poverty, no homelessness, no racial violence, and no gentrification battles. The psalmists often wrote of the new Jerusalem, God's city on earth. "Great is the LORD, and most worthy of praise, in the city of our God, his holy mountain" (Psalm 48:1). The new Jerusalem will represent the best this earthly city has to offer . . . and then some.

For one, there will be a rich diversity present in the heavenly city. The inhabitants will be from "every tribe and language and people and nation" (Revelation 5:9)—much like the city of Jerusalem today. Except in the heavenly city, these groups will not live in distinct districts with visible or invisible marks of separation. They will all live together, united in praise of Jesus Christ. The prophet Isaiah offered the following forecast when he wrote:

> [1] *I will sing for the one I love*
> *a song about his vineyard:*
> *My loved one had a vineyard*
> *on a fertile hillside.*
> [2] *He dug it up and cleared it of stones*
> *and planted it with the choicest vines.*
> *He built a watchtower in it*
> *and cut out a winepress as well.*
> *Then he looked for a crop of good grapes,*
> *but it yielded only bad fruit.*
> [3] *"Now you dwellers in Jerusalem and people of Judah,*
> *judge between me and my vineyard.*
> [4] *What more could have been done for my vineyard*
> *than I have done for it?*
> *When I looked for good grapes,*
> *why did it yield only bad?*
> [5] *Now I will tell you*
> *what I am going to do to my vineyard:*

I will take away its hedge,
and it will be destroyed;
I will break down its wall,
and it will be trampled.
⁶ I will make it a wasteland,
neither pruned nor cultivated,
and briers and thorns will grow there.
I will command the clouds
not to rain on it."
⁷ The vineyard of the Lᴏʀᴅ Almighty
is the nation of Israel,
and the people of Judah
are the vines he delighted in.
And he looked for justice, but saw bloodshed;
for righteousness, but heard cries of distress.

Isaiah 5:1–7

Isaiah echoes themes that are found in the book of Revelation. In both, God is portrayed as longing for a harmonious relationship with his people. Just as Isaiah depicts a vineyard tended by God that yields wild grapes due to Israel's disobedience, so Revelation reveals a world marred by sin and rebellion against God (see Revelation 20:7–10).

Both passages also hold the promise of restoration. In Revelation 21:1–4, we see a new heaven and a new earth where God dwells among his people and there is no more death, mourning, or pain. The imagery of a new Jerusalem adorned as a bride parallels Isaiah's vision of a renewed earth, lush with fertility and abundance. Both passages point to a future reality where God's redemptive work transforms the brokenness of the world into a paradise where righteousness reigns, drawing believers into an eternal communion with their creator.

The city will also be marked with beauty. It will be a sight to behold! God's glory will give the city its light, making it radiant as a precious stone (see Revelation 21:11, 21–23). The streets will be made of pure gold. When you read John's words, it's as if he is searching for a way to describe it. He is using the best of what this earth has to offer and saying that those things will be commonplace in heaven. Can you imagine that type of beauty?

Finally, like any earthly city, the new Jerusalem will be filled with people. A great multitude will call the city their home (see Revelation 7:9). In a previous lesson, we discussed how the way to heaven is via a small gate and narrow road, and that "only a few find it" (Matthew 7:14). This is certainly true at any moment in time. But the cumulative total of all who have trusted Jesus throughout history is a great multitude that no one can count. It is a great cloud of witnesses that testify to God's saving work (see Hebrews 12:1–2).

5. What does God say about the way he had cared for his "vineyard" in Isaiah 5:1–7? What was God saying about the way he had cared for his people?

6. What aspects of the new Jerusalem will be similar to cities on earth? What aspects will be decidedly different from anything encountered on earth?

A New Purpose

At first glance, the prospect of residing in a perfect city sounds appealing. Who wouldn't be drawn to the idea of dwelling in a flawless environment? Yet a question soon arises: *What will the inhabitants of this city actually be doing?* Even in the most idyllic setting, prolonged periods of inactivity lead to boredom. So how will God's people pass their time in eternity?

The consistent message conveyed throughout the Bible is that the primary occupation of God's people in this perfect city will be worship. This notion is prominently depicted in the book of Revelation, where multitudes are portrayed engaging in continuous praise and adoration of the Almighty. Their existence is characterized by a perpetual celebration of the sovereignty and majesty of God, who reigns supreme for all to witness.

However, as we think about worship as an occupation, we will likely need to expand our perceptions. Worship transcends the confines of traditional religious practices such as singing songs and raising hands in church. While these expressions are valuable aspects of worship, true worship encompasses every facet of our lives. It extends beyond the walls of a sanctuary and permeates into the mundane moments of our existence. In essence, worship is about glorifying God in everything we do, whether it is through our work, our creativity, or our interactions with others. Paul had this idea of worship in mind when he wrote:

> [15] *Let the peace of Christ rule in your hearts, since as members of one body you were called to peace. And be thankful.* [16] *Let the message of Christ dwell among you richly as you teach and admonish one another with all wisdom through psalms, hymns, and songs from the Spirit, singing to God with gratitude in your hearts.* [17] *And whatever you do, whether in word or deed, do it all in the name of the Lord Jesus, giving thanks to God the Father through him. . . .* [23] *Whatever you do, work at it with all your heart, as working for the Lord, not for human masters,* [24] *since you know that you will receive an inheritance from the Lord as a reward. It is the Lord Christ you are serving.*
>
> Colossians 3:15–17, 23–24

When we approach our tasks with excellence and integrity—working at them with all our hearts as if working for the Lord—we are offering them as acts of worship to God. Our creativity becomes a means of reflecting the beauty and complexity of our creator. Even the simplest acts of kindness and compassion can be elevated to acts of worship when done with a heart that seeks to honor God. In this way, worship becomes a holistic lifestyle where every aspect of our being is devoted to bringing glory and honor to the one who deserves it all.

So, as we think about how we will spend eternity, we need to think about it holistically. We need to think about heavenly worship as the perfecting of how we should worship now. In the new heavens and new earth, everything will be redeemed, including our worship.

7. How does this picture of heaven compare with how you have typically thought about it?

8. What comes to mind when you think about worship? How would you define worship?

REFLECT

Worship is a whole life orientation to God's glory (see Romans 12:1–2). Everything we do in response to God's greatness is an act of worship. This means that anything and everything we do in heaven as a response to God's greatness will be worship as well. Since we will no longer be able to sin, then anything that we do will be appropriate worship to God.

We can get a sense of what this might look like by considering what happened back at creation. "The LORD God took the man and put him in the Garden of Eden to work it and take care of it" (Genesis 2:15). God gave Adam and Eve a key task in the world that he just created. Certainly, he could have done the task himself. He could have built a world that did not need any cultivation or care. Instead, he made a world that allowed the first couple to use their gifts and abilities to harness the latent potential of that world in order to show off his glory.

Our work in heaven will likely follow this same pattern. We will cultivate and care for the new heavens and new earth that God has made. We will do so without the impact of sin. We will leverage artistry, creativity, and skill to continually tap into the great work of God and explore his glory. As we worship in this way, we will have the added benefit of bodies and minds that work perfectly and are not limited in the way they are on earth.

In the new heavens and new earth, everything we hoped we could have accomplished on this present earth will be realized. All our hopes and dreams—to the degree they are aligned with God's best—will be possible in the new earth. The good news in this is that we do not have to get it all done now! We do not have to put all of the pressure on ourselves to squeeze every ounce out of life. There will be plenty of time for that in eternity.

Furthermore, we will get to spend our time with others who are worshiping God in this same way. All those people from "every tribe and language and people and nation" will join us. This is why the local church matters. It's a picture of heaven. In the church, we partner with others to use our gifts to care for the world that God has made, including the people he has put in this world. When we pray that life on earth would look like heaven, the manifestation of this reality is among the people of God in the church. The church is a tiny microcosm of heaven, placed here on earth to give us a sense of our heavenly destiny. We should care about and invest in the local church because it is what we will be doing for all eternity.

God desires for the local church to serve as a reflection (albeit an imperfect one) of the fellowship that will be found in heaven. One way the church can do this is by encouraging its members to contribute their own unique gifts and talents without fear of insecurity or dominance. Just as the body has many parts with different functions, so too the church encompasses individuals with varied skills and perspectives. Each member should recognize his or her intrinsic value within the larger community, fostering an environment where collaboration flourishes. In this way, the church embodies the essence of heaven, where unity is forged through love and diversity is cherished as a testament to the richness of God's creation.

God's grace empowers the church to continually strive toward embodying the heavenly ideals of love, peace, and reconciliation, thereby offering glimpses of heaven to a world in need of hope. As the local church embraces its diversity and operates as a unified body, it becomes a living testimony to the transformative power of God's love. Through genuine relationships, compassionate service, and unwavering commitment to justice, the church becomes a light in the darkness, illuminating the path toward a future where the perfect peace of heaven will be fully realized. In every act of kindness, every gesture of reconciliation, and every expression of solidarity, the local church brings heaven a little closer to earth, reminding us of the boundless possibilities when we strive to live in alignment with God's vision for humanity.

9. If you could do anything to make the world a better place, what would that be? How do you think this passion will translate to your tasks in heaven?

10. How is your local church a picture of heaven on earth? What are some ways that you can work to make your church reflect more of heaven on earth?

CLOSE

Our heavenly home and city, prefigured in the local church, are indeed another source of profound hope for us in this life. Just as we anticipate the joy of reuniting with loved ones after a long journey, so we can endure and persevere through life's trials with the knowledge that something infinitely greater awaits us. The yearning for our heavenly home parallels the longing for our ideal earthly home—a place where love and acceptance abound and where pain and suffering will be no more. As members of God's family, this anticipation should stir within us a deep longing for the fulfillment of God's promises, knowing that heaven, prepared by the hands of God, will surpass any earthly dwelling we have ever known.

Our lives on this earth often mirror the experiences of travel, with its ups and downs and moments of uncertainty and revelation. However, just as the traveler remains steadfast in the hope of reaching his or her destination, so too are God's people called to persevere in the assurance of their heavenly inheritance. Even in the midst of life's most arduous challenges, we find solace in the knowledge that our trials are temporary and that an eternal home awaits us where every tear will be wiped away and every sorrow turned to joy. This hopeful expectation sustains us, infusing our journey with purpose and fortitude as we press onward toward the heavenly city, our hearts set ablaze with anticipation of the glory that awaits.

So as we journey through this life, let us hold fast to the hope of our heavenly home, allowing it to anchor our souls in times of uncertainty and despair. Just as the local church serves as a foretaste of heaven on earth, so too does our anticipation of eternity sustain us through life's trials. May we, as God's children, live with the assurance that our true home lies beyond this earthly realm, where we will dwell in the presence of our creator for all eternity, surrounded by the boundless love and beauty of heaven.

11. What longing do you have today to experience your eternal home?

12. What is one way that God is sustaining you on this journey through life?

Lesson Six

THE BEGINNING AND END

The L*ord* *will be king over the whole earth. On that day there will be one* L*ord,* *and his name the only name.*

ZECHARIAH 14:9

But in keeping with his promise we are looking forward to a new heaven and a new earth, where righteousness dwells.

2 Peter 3:13

"I am the Alpha and the Omega, the First and the Last, the Beginning and the End."

REVELATION 22:13

WELCOME

As I mentioned previously, we are living in the middle of God's story. We weren't there when God made the world in the beginning, and unless Jesus returns in our lifetime, we won't be there when God writes the final chapter at the end. This reality can make it difficult for us to keep our focus on God's overall story instead of our temporal existence. We all have priorities that vie for our attention, relationships we want to maintain, jobs that require our focus, hobbies that bring us joy. We can go for days, weeks, or years without giving more than a cursory thought to God's mission.

Throughout history, people have spent an abundance of time and energy discussing how the world is going to end. From environmental theories to conspiracy theories, most believe that the days of this earth are numbered. Even within the church, pastors and scholars differ on their understanding of when and how God will bring his great story to a conclusion. God does not reveal all the details to us of how or when the end of the age will take place.

This can be disconcerting to us, because we like to know the details of anything that impacts our future. Perhaps this is why so many people get caught up in discussing matters that the biblical authors simply did not see the need to address. For instance, those who study the creation of the world often invest great effort in discussing the various scientific theories related to how God made all things. But this wasn't the main concern of the author of Genesis. He wrote the book to show readers that God created all things through the power of his word. All the other details that fascinate modern readers were not central to his concern.

Similarly, the biblical authors did not see the need to provide a detailed analysis of how God's story will ultimately come to an end. In fact, Jesus told his followers, "But about that day or hour no one knows, not even the angels in heaven, nor the Son, but only the Father" (Matthew 24:36). He provides a hint as to why a few verses later:

"So you also must be ready, because the Son of Man will come at an hour when you do not expect him" (verse 44).

Consider an example from everyday life. Imagine as a teenager that your parents leave you at home alone for the evening. They give you a speech before they leave, reminding you not to do anything stupid and instructing you to make sure you have vacuumed the rugs, cleaned your room, and taken out the garbage while they are out. They say that they will be home at 11:00 PM sharp and that you better be ready. What do you do?

Well, if you are like most teenagers, you do anything you want until 10:45 PM. Then, in the last fifteen minutes before your parents get home, you frantically scramble to get all your chores done and put the house together. Now imagine how the situation would be different if your mom and dad said they were going out to run a few errands and then gave you the chores to do. The dynamic would shift drastically. You would be more likely to get your tasks done sooner rather than later based on the fact your parents could return home at any time.

The same is true of Jesus' return. God knows that if he were to give his followers a specific time and date for this event, they would be more likely to procrastinate in pursuing their mission. They would rationalize that they had plenty of time to "clean house" when it comes to their own lives. So instead, God instructs his followers to remain constantly vigilant.

1. How should the uncertainty of Jesus' return impact his followers' lives?

2. In what ways are you living with an expectation of Jesus' imminent return?

READ

The Day of the Lord

Zechariah was an Old Testament prophet who ministered in Israel after the exile. The opening words of his prophecy state that he was active during "the eighth month of the second year" of King Darius I of Persia (Zechariah 1:1). At the time, the Persians were allowing the Jewish exiles who had been taken into captivity by the Babylonians to return to their homeland. Zechariah, along with his grandfather Iddo, were likely in the first group who returned.

Zechariah begins his prophecy with a proclamation and a promise from God: "'Return to me,' declares the LORD Almighty, 'and I will return to you'" (verse 3). The Lord was reminding the exiles of how their ancestors had rebelled against him and failed to turn from their "evil ways" and "evil practices" (verse 4). God says to them, "Did not my words and my decrees, which I commanded my servants and the prophets, overtake your ancestors?" (verse 6).

Zechariah writes that the people responded by vowing to not make the same mistakes of their forefathers. "Then they repented and said, 'The LORD Almighty has done to us what our ways and practices deserve, just as he determined to do'" (verse 6). The rest of the book contains Zechariah's prophecies from the Lord to this group of exiles who had repented.

In one of these messages, the prophet describes the events of what he refers to as the "Day of the Lord." This was a term used by many Old Testament prophets to describe a future time when God's "stored up" wrath would be released against evil. (Recall the illustration of the dam storing up water in lesson three.) Zechariah speaks of this day as being a period of great upheaval and judgment, as he relates in the following passage:

> ¹ *A day of the* LORD *is coming, Jerusalem, when your possessions will be plundered and divided up within your very walls.*
>
> ² *I will gather all the nations to Jerusalem to fight against it; the city will be captured, the houses ransacked, and the women raped. Half of the city will go into exile, but the rest of the people will not be taken from the city.* ³ *Then the* LORD *will go out and fight against those nations, as he fights on a day of battle.* ⁴ *On that day his feet will stand on the Mount of Olives, east of Jerusalem, and the Mount of Olives will be split in two from east to west, forming a great valley, with half of the mountain moving north and half moving south.* ⁵ *You will flee by my mountain valley, for it will extend to Azel. You will flee as you fled from the earthquake in the days of Uzziah king of Judah. Then the* LORD *my God will come, and all the holy ones with him.*
>
> ⁶ *On that day there will be neither sunlight nor cold, frosty darkness.* ⁷ *It will be a unique day—a day known only to the* LORD*—with no distinction between day and night. When evening comes, there will be light.*
>
> ⁸ *On that day living water will flow out from Jerusalem, half of it east to the Dead Sea and half of it west to the Mediterranean Sea, in summer and in winter.*
>
> ⁹ *The* LORD *will be king over the whole earth. On that day there will be one* LORD*, and his name the only name.*
>
> Zechariah 14:1–9

The opening words of Zephaniah's prophecy portray a bleak situation for God's people when the Day of the Lord begins. They will have their possessions plundered and divided up. All the nations of the world will gather against Jerusalem to fight against them. The city will be captured, and atrocities will be committed against its inhabitants. Half of the people will again be taken into exile . . . but the other half will remain as a remnant.

It is at this point, in the midst all the chaos, that God himself will intervene into his people's story. He will stand on the Mount of Olives, splitting it in two from east to west, and will usher in a new era of his divine kingship. This powerful imagery evokes a sense of both fear and hope, as it foretells the culmination of God's redemptive plan and his ultimate victory over all opposition. Zechariah's words serve as a poignant reminder of the Lord's sovereignty—inspiring followers of God to live in anticipation of when this ultimate victory will occur.

Jesus later revealed to his disciples that he would be the fulfillment of this prophecy. Standing on the Mount of Olives—not a mere coincidence—he proclaimed, "But in those days, following that distress [of the Day of the Lord]. . . . At that time people will see the Son of Man coming in clouds with great power and glory. And he will send his angels and gather his elect from the four winds, from the ends of the earth to the ends of the heavens" (Mark 13:24, 26–27).

Even though the date and time of when all these events will occur is uncertain, one thing is crystal clear: Jesus *will* return to finish his work to save sinners and fix the world. The writer of Hebrews puts it this way: "Christ was sacrificed once to take away the sins of many; and he will appear a second time, not to bear sin, but to bring salvation to those who are waiting for him" (Hebrews 9:28). John adds, "'Look, he is coming with the clouds,' and 'every eye will see him, even those who pierced him.' . . . So shall it be!" (Revelation 1:7).

Jesus will return a second time. When he does, his mission in this world will be both different and the same from his first appearance. It will be different in that Jesus is not coming again to deal with sins by dying a death to pay their penalty and to prove his victory by rising from the tomb. He has already accomplished that mission. He has fully paid the price for sin. However, his mission will be the same in that he is coming into the world to save.

3. How do you think the people of Jerusalem reacted when they heard Zechariah's prophecy of the coming Day of the Lord? What questions does it raise for you?

4. How would you describe Jesus' return to this world based on the prophecies found in Zechariah 14:1–9 and Christ's own words in Mark 13:24–31?

The Triumphant Return

Paul wrote to one group of believers, "Our citizenship is in heaven. And we eagerly await a Savior from there, the Lord Jesus Christ" (Philippians 3:20). Paul lived in eager expectation of Jesus' return. This anticipation was entrenched in the belief that it would herald the culmination of the salvation narrative that Christ had initiated during his earthly ministry.

Seen in this light, the second coming of Jesus is the final act in God's redemptive plan, wherein the restoration of humanity and creation reaches its consummation. Jesus' first arrival on earth initiated the process of salvation, offering humanity redemption through his death and resurrection. However, it is through his return that this salvation will reach its full realization. At that juncture, God's people will be perfected and dwell in a realm devoid of sin—with Satan, sin, and death defeated for eternity. Christ's return thus represents his ultimate victory over evil and the establishment of God's eternal kingdom, where righteousness reigns supreme.

Jesus' return signifies the dawn of a new era where the effects of sin are eradicated and humanity experiences the fullness of God's glory. The completion of salvation initiated by Jesus' first coming finds its ultimate expression in the second coming, underscoring the continuity and coherence of God's salvific plan throughout history. As believers await this climactic moment, which John describes in the following passage, they are called to live in anticipation and readiness, striving to embody the values of God's kingdom as they look forward to that day:

> [11] *I saw heaven standing open and there before me was a white horse, whose rider is called Faithful and True. With justice he judges and wages war.* [12] *His eyes are like blazing fire, and on his head are many crowns. He has a name written on him that no one knows but he himself.* [13] *He is dressed in a robe dipped in blood, and his name is the Word of God.* [14] *The armies of heaven were following him, riding on white horses and dressed in fine linen, white and clean.* [15] *Coming out of his mouth is a sharp sword with which to strike down the nations. "He will rule them with an iron scepter." He treads the winepress of the fury of the wrath of God Almighty.* [16] *On his robe and on his thigh he has this name written:*
>
> *KING OF KINGS AND LORD OF LORDS.*
>
> [17] *And I saw an angel standing in the sun, who cried in a loud voice to all the birds flying in midair, "Come, gather together for the great supper of God,* [18] *so that you may eat the flesh of kings, generals, and the mighty, of horses and their riders, and the flesh of all people, free and slave, great and small."*
>
> [19] *Then I saw the beast and the kings of the earth and their armies gathered together to wage war against the rider on the horse and his army.* [20] *But the beast was captured, and with it the false prophet who had performed the signs on its behalf. With these signs he had deluded those who had received the mark of the beast and worshiped its image. The two of them were thrown alive into the fiery lake of burning sulfur.* [21] *The rest were killed with the sword coming out of the mouth of the rider on the horse, and all the birds gorged themselves on their flesh.*
>
> Revelation 19:11–21

John here relates the awe-inspiring imagery of the triumphant return of Christ that he witnessed in his vision. Jesus is depicted as a conquering king with eyes of "blazing fire," wearing "many crowns," and dressed in "a robe dipped in blood." He and the armies of heaven are riding on "white horses." In ancient times, victorious Roman generals would enter the cities they conquered in chariots drawn by white horses—and the same will be true of Jesus' heavenly forces. Christ "treads the winepress of the fury of the wrath of God Almighty," an image that recalls Isaiah 5:1-7. The "beast" and the "false prophet," who are agents of Satan's evil forces, are captured and "thrown alive into the fiery lake of burning sulfur."

Later, John tells us that Satan, "the devil, who deceived them, was thrown into the lake of burning sulfur, where the beast and the false prophet had been thrown" (Revelation 20:10). Jesus' victory over Satan and his allies is thus complete. God's redemptive plan that he established after the fall has been fulfilled. His kingdom has been established forever.

As we reflect on this powerful depiction, we are reminded of the sovereignty and power of Jesus Christ, who reigns supreme over all creation. In the face of adversity and turmoil, John's description of Jesus' return serves as a source of hope and assurance for believers, affirming that God's purposes will ultimately prevail and that justice will be fully realized. As we await the fulfillment of these prophetic promises, we are called to live with faith and perseverance, knowing that our ultimate victory is assured through the triumph of Christ.

5. What images especially stand out to you in John's description of Jesus?

6. Why is it important for you personally to know that God will triumph over all the evil in this world and that his justice will ultimately prevail?

Waiting in Active Obedience

Hope is a word that is often used today to express a number of emotions of varying degrees. We hope that our flight will be on time. We hope that a medical checkup will go well. We hope that a loved one will return home safely to us. These are all examples of "worldly" hope.

Followers of Jesus have an additional kind of hope—an "otherworldly" kind. We have the hope that what God has promised to us will come to pass. Unlike the worldly kind of hope, where we are just wishing that something will one day happen, the hope that God provides is sure and certain. We can have a confident expectation that God will deliver on his promises. This is true as it relates to God's promise that he will defeat the enemy and sin will be no more. It is also true as it relates to his promise that he will take his followers to live with him forever.

In the meantime . . . we wait.

If we are honest, none of us really like the idea of waiting. We want things to happen now. Waiting is uncertain. Waiting can be unsettling. Waiting can be dull.

We wait for a job promotion. We wait for that other person to ask us out. We wait to get our tax refund in the mail. Often, the idea of waiting denotes sitting back in anticipation for something coming that we cannot control. We tend to think of waiting in a passive sense. However, here again, we need to challenge such perceptions of waiting as it relates to anticipating Jesus' return.

God does not call us to passively stand by while the clock ticks down. No, the waiting that we are called to do is active, as Peter describes in the following passage:

> ¹⁰ *But the day of the Lord will come like a thief. The heavens will disappear with a roar; the elements will be destroyed by fire, and the earth and everything done in it will be laid bare.*
> ¹¹ *Since everything will be destroyed in this way, what kind of people ought you to be? You ought to live holy and godly lives* ¹² *as you look forward to the day of God and speed its coming. That day will bring about the destruction of the heavens by fire, and the elements will melt in the heat.* ¹³ *But in keeping with his promise we are looking forward to a new heaven and a new earth, where righteousness dwells.*
> ¹⁴ *So then, dear friends, since you are looking forward to this, make every effort to be found spotless, blameless and at peace with him.*
>
> 2 Peter 3:10–14

The kind of waiting that Peter describes is like the waiting you do when your wedding day is right around the corner. It's the waiting you do the week of the championship game. The anticipation drives you to prepare. In the first scenario, you are doing things like picking a venue, hiring a photographer, and picking out a wedding dress. In the latter, you are going to practice, watching what you eat, analyzing tape of the opposition's tendencies, and honing your game plan. Brides and ballplayers don't wait passively. They are engaged and active.

Christians wait in the same way. They pursue holiness and godliness and are caught up in God's mission in the world. They wait in active obedience.

Peter says that people who live in this way hasten the day of Jesus' coming. They "speed its coming." No one knows exactly how this happens, but somehow in God's plan, the faithfulness of his people has an impact on when Jesus returns. One possible explanation is found in Matthew 24, where Jesus is describing some of the events that will occur before he returns. Among other things, he says, "This gospel of the kingdom will be preached in the whole world as a testimony to all nations, and then the end will come" (verse 14).

In other words, the gospel—the good news of salvation—will go to the ends of the earth before the end comes. So, as followers of Jesus are faithful to declare the gospel among the nations, they hasten the fulfillment of this prophecy. They obey Jesus' command to "make disciples of all nations" (Matthew 28:19). They actively take part in his mission.

7. When you hear the words *hope* and *waiting*, what immediately comes to mind?

8. How would you describe the kind of *hope* that followers of Jesus have? How would you describe the kind of waiting discussed in 2 Peter 3:10-14?

REFLECT

Followers of Jesus remain invested in his mission. God's story, as told in the Bible, reminds us that this mission is the only thing that truly matters. While our lives seem important, especially to us, God's story began long before we were born and will continue long after we die.

In the final chapter of the Bible, God declares that he is "the Alpha and the Omega" (Revelation 22:13). He uses the first and last letters of the Greek alphabet to show that he started the story and will finish it. As he said to Moses, he is the great "I AM" (Exodus 3:14). He was, is, and always will be at work to fulfill his mission. Our God is eternal, and nothing and no one will ever deter him from accomplishing his divine purposes in the world.

We witness this truth at work throughout God's story. In the *Beginning*, God created a good and peaceful world. He fashioned people in his image and commanded them to multiply and fill the earth with image-bearing worshipers of himself. They were meant to rule over his world so that his greatness would be seen and known.

However, people chose an alternative path. Instead of submitting to God's plan, they staged a *Revolt* that plunged the world into sin. God judged them in their rebellion, but he did not abandon them completely—nor did he abandon his plans for them to rule and reign. Instead, he set out on a mission to save sinners and put the world back together again.

Part of this plan involved God calling out a group of *People* to serve as an example to the world. He gave this group of people, the Israelites, his law, the temple, the sacrificial system, and the Promised Land to establish them as a light to the nations. The Israelites were meant to showcase God's grace to the world, but they also chose to rebel against God. So, ultimately, the Lord allowed foreign nations to invade and carry his people away from their land.

However, even in their exile, God did not abandon his people. He promised that they would one day return to their homeland and be restored to him. Then, in the fullness of time, God revealed his ultimate plan for the restoration and return of all people. He sent Jesus, who was literally God-in-the-flesh, to dwell with people on the earth and be their *Savior*.

In truth, it was God's design all along to send his Son into the world to do what Adam and the Israelites had been incapable of doing. Jesus lived a perfect life of obedience to God. He then died the death that sinners deserved to receive because of their rebellion and sin. Jesus then rose from the grave—victorious over Satan, sin, and death.

Jesus' sacrifice made a way for all people to be brought back into a right relationship with God. Those who chose to accept Christ's offer of salvation and put their hope in him became members of his *Church*. This community of believers accepted God's call to declare and demonstrate his mission to the world. This mission will continue until Jesus returns, establishes his rule over the earth, and perfectly restores his people to worship him rightly *Forever*.

This is God's story . . . and we are now a part of that story.

9. God described himself to Moses as being "I AM WHO I AM" (Exodus 3:14) and to John as being "the Beginning and the End" (Revelation 22:13). What do each of these names reveal about God's nature? Why do you think God described himself in these ways?

10. As you look back on God's overarching story, how has the Lord demonstrated his mercy to people throughout time? How has he demonstrated his mercy to you personally?

CLOSE

Our hope in creating *Forever*, and all the studies in *The Jesus Bible Study Series*, is to extend an invitation for you to immerse yourself in the vast and brilliant story of

God's redemptive plan. As you continue to engage with this narrative, it is our prayer that it becomes the dominant story in your life, shaping your priorities, passions, and life mission. Indeed, the depth and beauty of this story is inexhaustible and requires a lifetime of exploration to fully grasp its implications. Each stage of life offers new insights and opportunities for growth as the Holy Spirit reveals different themes and truths that resonate with your circumstances.

As you delve deeper into God's story, you will discover that there is always more to learn and experience. Every encounter with Scripture unveils new layers of grace and truth, leading you to "grow in the grace and knowledge of our Lord and Savior Jesus Christ" (2 Peter 3:18). The journey of faith is marked by continual transformation and growth as you allow the Holy Spirit to illuminate your heart and mind with the profound realities of God's love and redemption. With each revelation, you are called to respond faithfully, allowing the story of Jesus to shape not only your beliefs but also your actions and relationships.

Ultimately, your mission as a follower of Christ is to bear witness to the transformative power of his love and then invite others to join in the glorious privilege of knowing and serving the Savior. Until he returns, may we all remain steadfast in our commitment to this mission, faithfully living out the story of Jesus in our lives and extending his invitation to all who will listen. In this journey of faith, may we be empowered by the Spirit to grow in grace, deepen in knowledge, and reflect more fully the love and character of our Lord and Savior.

11. How will you continue to grow in your experience with God after completing this study?

12. What is God calling you to do next? Who can you share God's story with this coming week?

NEXT

During our time in these six lessons of *Forever,* we have explored how God has promised that his faithful followers will one day reside with him in eternity. For this reason, we can stand firm in the face of anything that the enemy throws at us in this life. We examined how we can live on this earth while maintaining a heaven-focused perspective. We also saw that the road to eternal life, while open to all, is difficult and narrow. Finally, we discussed the Bible's promises about our future resurrection, about the heavenly home and city that God has built for us, and about the hope we have that God will one day forever defeat the forces of evil that assail us.

Now that you have been given a glimpse of what God has promised you at the end of his story, it might be a good time to revisit what he promised back in the beginning. Remember that God's plan of redemption has not changed! He created humans in his own image. He made them unique in fundamental ways. He charged them to take dominion over all creation. He made them male and female and designed them to live in community, modeling the community that has forever existed between the Father, the Son, and the Holy Spirit. Now that you know the end of the story, you will gain new insights as you again explore how it all began.

Thank you for taking this journey! Stay the course. God has a lot more that he wants to do in your life!

LEADER'S GUIDE

Thank you for your willingness to lead your group through this study. What you have chosen to do is valuable and will make a great difference in the lives of others. The rewards of being a leader are different from those of participating, and we hope that as you lead you will find your own walk with Jesus deepened by the experience.

The lessons in this study guide are suitable for church classes, Bible studies, and small groups. Each lesson is structured to provoke thought and help you grow in your knowledge and understanding of Christ. There are multiple components in this section that can help you structure your lessons and discussion time, so make sure you read and consider each one.

BEFORE YOU BEGIN

Before your first meeting, make sure the group members have a copy of this study guide so they can follow along and have their answers written out ahead of time. Alternately, you can hand out the study guides at your first meeting and give the group members some time to look over the material and ask any preliminary questions. During your first meeting, be sure to send a sheet of paper around the room and have the members write down their name, phone number, and email address so you can keep in touch with them during the week.

Generally, the ideal size for a group is eight to ten people, which will ensure that everyone has enough time to participate in discussions. If you have more people, you might want to break up the main group into smaller subgroups. Encourage those who show up at the first meeting to commit to attending the duration of the study. This will help the group members get to know one another, create stability for the group, and help you, as the leader, know how to best prepare each week.

Try to initiate a free-flowing discussion as you go through each lesson. Invite group members to bring any questions they have or insights they discover as they go through the content to the next meeting, especially if they were unsure of the meaning of some parts of the lesson. Be prepared to discuss the biblical truth that relates to each topic in the study.

WEEKLY PREPARATION

As the group leader, here are a few things you can do to prepare for each meeting:

- Make sure you understand the content of the lesson so you know how to structure group time and are prepared to lead group discussion.
- Depending on how much time you have each week, you may not be able to reflect on every question. Select specific questions that you feel will evoke the best discussion.
- At the end of your discussion, take prayer requests from your group members and pray for each other.

STRUCTURING THE DISCUSSION TIME

It is up to you to keep track of the time and keep things on schedule. You might want to set a timer for each question that you discuss so both you and the group members know when your time is up. (There are some good phone apps for timers that play a gentle chime or other pleasant sound instead of a disruptive noise.)

Don't be concerned if the group members are quiet or slow to share. People are often quiet when they are pulling together their ideas, and this might be a new experience for them. Just ask a question and let it hang in the air until someone shares. You can then say, "Thank you. What about others? What thoughts came to you?"

If you need help in organizing your time when planning your group Bible study, the following schedule, for sixty minutes and ninety minutes, can give you a structure for the lesson:

	60 Minutes	90 Minutes
Welcome: Arrive and get settled	5 minutes	10 minutes
Message: Review the lesson	15 minutes	25 minutes
Discussion: Discuss study questions	35 minutes	45 minutes
Prayer: Pray together and dismiss	5 minutes	10 minutes

GROUP DYNAMICS

Leading a group through *Forever* will prove to be highly rewarding both to you and your group members. But you still may encounter challenges along the way! Discussions can get off track. Group members may not be sensitive to the needs and ideas of others. Some might worry they will be expected to talk about matters that make them feel awkward. Others may express comments that result in disagreements. To help ease this strain on you and the group, consider the following ground rules:

- When someone raises a question or comment that is off the main topic, suggest you deal with it another time, or, if you feel led to go in that direction, let the group know you will be spending some time discussing it.

- If someone asks a question that you don't know how to answer, admit it and move on. At your discretion, feel free to invite group members to comment on questions that call for personal experience.

- If you find one or two people are dominating the discussion time, direct a few questions to others in the group. Outside the main group time, ask the more dominating members to help you draw out the quieter ones. Work to make them a part of the solution instead of the problem.

- When a disagreement occurs, encourage the group members to process the matter in love. Encourage those on opposite sides to restate what they heard the other side say about the matter, and then invite each side to evaluate if that perception is accurate. Lead the group in examining other Scriptures related to the topic and look for common ground.

When any of these issues arise, encourage your group members to follow these words from the Bible: "Love one another" (John 13:34), "If it is possible, as far as it depends on you, live at peace with everyone" (Romans 12:18), "Whatever is true . . . noble . . . right . . . if anything is excellent or praiseworthy—think about such things" (Philippians 4:8), and "Be quick to listen, slow to speak and slow to become angry" (James 1:19). This will make your group time more rewarding and beneficial for everyone who attends.

Thank you again for your willingness to lead your group. May God reward your efforts and dedication, equip you to guide your group in the weeks ahead, and make your time together fruitful for his kingdom.

ABOUT THE AUTHORS

Aaron Coe has spent more than twenty years working in the nonprofit and philanthropic space. Much of that time was spent in New York City in the years after 9/11, helping with revitalization efforts. Aaron served as vice president at North American Mission Board, providing strategic guidance and leadership. He has also worked with organizations like Passion, illumiNations, Food for the Hungry, the Ethics and Religious Liberty Commission, and many others. Aaron has a Ph.D. in Applied Theology and teaches at Dallas Theological Seminary. He is the founder of Future City Now, which seeks to help visionary leaders maximize their influence in the world. Additionally, Aaron served as the General Editor of *The Jesus Bible*. Aaron lives in Atlanta with his wife, Carmen, and their four children.

Matthew Rogers holds a Ph.D. in Applied Theology and teaches and writes on Christian mission, ministry, and discipleship. Notably, Matthew served as the lead writer for the bestselling *The Jesus Bible*. He and his wife, Sarah, and their five children live in Greenville, South Carolina, where Matthew serves as the pastor of Christ Fellowship Cherrydale.

The Jesus Bible Study Series

Beginnings
ISBN 9780310154983

Revolt
ISBN 9780310155003

People
ISBN 9780310155027

Savior
ISBN 9780310155041

Church
ISBN 9780310155065

Forever
ISBN 9780310155089
On sale September 2024

Available wherever books are sold

The Jesus Bible

sixty-six books. one story. all about one name.

The Jesus Bible, NIV & ESV editions, with feature essays from Louie Giglio, Max Lucado, John Piper, and Randy Alcorn, as well as profound yet accessible study features will help you meet Jesus throughout Scripture.

- 350 full page articles
- 700 side-bar articles
- Book introductions
- Room for journaling

The Jesus Bible Journal, NIV
Study individual books of the Bible featuring lined journal space and commentary from *The Jesus Bible.*

- 14 journals covering 30 books of the Bible
- 2 boxed sets (OT & NT)

TheJesusBible.com